Contents

Foreword

By the Secretary of State for Culture, Media and Sport and the Minister for Culture, Welsh Language and Sport, Welsh Assembly Government

The historic environment matters to all of us. It tells us about who we are and where we have come from. It gives identity to our villages, towns and cities. It has shaped the distinctive character of our countryside.

People recognise and value the importance of the historic environment. It makes where they live and work special. They look after historic assets in their care. They participate through volunteering, study, activities and events. They visit historic buildings and sites in huge numbers.

The heritage protection system is about how we protect and sustain this essential resource, both for us today and for future generations.

We know how important this is. People care passionately about how their historic environment is preserved. They want a system that provides the right levels of protection. They want to be involved in decisions about their heritage and about how we manage change.

But alongside this support, there is an appetite for reform. People want a heritage protection system that is simple to understand and to use. They want a more open system that enables individuals and communities to make their voice heard. And they want a clearer role for the heritage in wider policy – they want to see the historic environment at the heart of planning, of regeneration, of environmental stewardship, and of building sustainable communities.

Since our public consultation in 2003, the context within which we operate has changed. We are reforming our planning systems to make them more efficient and more responsive. We are committed to a new relationship between central and local Government, and between local Government and citizens. We are continuing to make our public services more efficient and to cut red tape. In Wales, the Government of Wales Act 2006 means more powers for the National Assembly and the Assembly Government.

The sector itself is changing. We have carried out ground-breaking new research that underlines the popularity of the historic environment. We are tackling the barriers to participation among certain groups. We have modernised delivery structures. And we have continued to identify, research and protect our historic assets.

Department for Culture, Media and Sport
Welsh Assembly Government

Heritage Protection for the 21st Century

Presented to Parliament by the
Secretary of State for Culture, Media and Sport
By Command of Her Majesty, March 2007

Cm 7057

This White Paper responds to the public call for change, and to this changing policy context. It sets out our vision for a new heritage protection system. Our proposals are based on a unified vision of the historic environment that enables a simpler and more efficient system. They are focussed on opening up heritage protection to greater public scrutiny and involvement. And they recognise that heritage protection needs to be an integral part of a planning system that can deliver sustainable communities.

Developing this White Paper has been a collaborative process. In particular, we have worked closely with colleagues in the Scottish Executive and in Northern Ireland to develop proposals for changes to the marine historic environment. We are enormously grateful for this work, which will mean bring real improvements to the protection of our marine heritage.

The White Paper presents a challenging agenda for change for all of us. For central Government, for local Government, and for the sector. But the benefits are great. At a time of rapid development and change, our reforms will put heritage protection on a sound footing for the future. We look forward to working with you to deliver our vision.

Rt Hon. Tessa Jowell MP
Secretary of State for Culture, Media and Sport

Alun Pugh AM
Minister for Culture, Welsh Language and Sport

Executive summary

The proposals in this White Paper reflect the importance of the heritage protection system in preserving our heritage for people to enjoy now and in the future. They are based around three core principles:

- Developing a unified approach to the historic environment;
- Maximising opportunities for inclusion and involvement; and
- Supporting sustainable communities by putting the historic environment at the heart of an effective planning system.

DEVELOPING A UNIFIED APPROACH TO THE HISTORIC ENVIRONMENT

One of the key strengths of the historic environment is its depth and diversity – it encompasses everything from an iron-age hill fort to the Severn and Wye bridges. But this diversity has also led to some unhelpful distinctions, to divisions between buildings and archaeological remains, or between urban and rural heritage.

The heritage protection system in England and Wales has reflected and reinforced these distinctions. It has developed separate systems for dealing with different aspects of the historic environment and a range of professionals to operate these systems. As a consequence, the regime we have today can be perceived as complicated and hard to understand. It can be bureaucratic and burdensome. A lack of integration can mean that heritage issues may fail to carry the weight they should in wider policy debates.

Our vision is for a unified heritage protection system that is easy to understand and to use. To achieve this, we will:

- Provide a unified legislative framework for heritage protection that removes current distinctions to deliver a system that works for the whole historic environment.
- Build on this new legislative framework by creating a single system for national designation and consents and encouraging greater unification at local level.

MAXIMISING OPPORTUNITIES FOR INCLUSION AND INVOLVEMENT

Levels of public participation in the historic environment are high, and are rising. Whether through visiting, volunteering, or studying, substantial numbers of people choose to access or care for heritage in their free time. While participation rates are lower amongst people from ethnic minorities, with disabilities or from lower socio-economic groups, levels of engagement are good compared to other parts of the cultural sector, and improving them further remains a top priority for Government.

There is a positive story to tell, but there is scope to go further. The heritage protection system should make maximum use of opportunities to engage communities. The system can be perceived as opaque and complex, and as something designed to meet the needs of professionals rather than users.

Our vision is for a heritage protection system that is understandable and accessible, that engages the public in decisions on protection, and provides wide opportunities for involvement for individuals, owners, and community groups. To achieve this, we will:

- Open up the designation system to greater consultation and scrutiny and promote a debate on what we should protect in future.
- Provide the public with better information about how the system works and why things are protected.
- Encourage local authorities and local communities to identify and protect their local heritage.
- Provide people with better access to improved information about the historic environment around them.

DELIVERING SUSTAINABLE COMMUNITIES BY PUTTING THE HISTORIC ENVIRONMENT AT THE HEART OF AN EFFECTIVE PLANNING SYSTEM

The historic environment is an essential element of building sustainable communities. Whether through traditional building styles, ancient street patterns, or historic green spaces, heritage provides communities with a sense of identity and place. The effective re-use of historic buildings can provide a focus for regeneration and economic development and can ensure the sustainable use of resources.

The Government is in the process of a major programme of planning reform designed to promote sustainable communities. The reforms are based on plan-led development that can deliver greater certainty while ensuring input from local communities. They aim to create a system that is faster and more efficient, and that is operated by a skilled and resourced workforce. The recent Barker Review of Land Use Planning has called for further reforms to ensure greater flexibility, responsiveness and efficiency in the system, and a Planning White Paper is due shortly.

Heritage protection is an integral part of the planning system. Development pressures continue to increase and demands on the planning system are growing. In order to ensure effective protection for heritage, it is essential that we promote the importance of the historic environment within planning, and bring the heritage protection system in line with ongoing planning reforms. To do this, we will:

- Speed up the designation system and make it more efficient.
- Join up and streamline the consent process to reduce bureaucracy and make it more efficient.
- Consider introducing new tools for local planning authorities and developers to address heritage in major developments.
- Provide the means for devolving greater responsibility to local planning authorities so they can manage the historic environment alongside other planning responsibilities.

There is much about the current heritage protection system that works well. It has enabled us to manage the historic environment over more than a century of rapid change and has ensured the protection and preservation of some of the most important examples of our heritage. It is operated by a highly-skilled and committed workforce and supported by hundreds of thousands of volunteers. Our reforms are intended to build on the best of what we have to ensure a system that can respond to future challenges.

This is a White Paper for England and Wales and for the United Kingdom. The first part of the White Paper sets out legislative change and implementation arrangements for England. The second part covers implementation arrangements for Wales. The third part covers legislative change affecting the marine historic environment across the United Kingdom.

The proposals in this White Paper are the product of extensive consultation with the sector, and of close collaboration between the Department for Culture, Media and Sport, the Department for Communities and Local Government, the Department for Environment, Food and Rural Affairs, the devolved administrations and English Heritage. We will seek an opportunity for new legislation to implement our proposals at the earliest opportunity. In the meantime, we are also asking for views on three further options for change. These are summarised in Part 4.

SUMMARY OF RECOMMENDATIONS

We will promote a new holistic approach towards the historic environment by creating a single designation regime that is simple and easy to understand. To do this:

- We will create a single system for national designation to replace listing, scheduling and registering.
- All national designation decisions will be made on the basis of special architectural, historic or archaeological interest.
- We will make designation decisions easier to understand by publishing new detailed selection criteria for national and local designation.
- We will devolve responsibility for national designation in England to English Heritage.

We will improve designation by involving the public in decisions about what is protected and how, and by making the process simpler and quicker. To do this:

- We will involve the public in shaping a new programme of national designation.
- We will create new Registers of Historic Buildings and Sites of England and Wales to replace existing lists and schedules.
- We will introduce simpler and clearer designation records and improve public access to these records through new internet portals.
- We will open up the system by introducing new consultation and appeal processes.
- We will introduce interim protection for historic assets.
- We will speed up the system and deliver designation decisions faster.

We will support sustainable communities by putting the historic environment at the heart of an effective planning system. To do this:

- We will streamline regulation by merging Listed Building Consent and Scheduled Monument Consent, and by consulting on the merging of Conservation Area Consent with planning permission.
- We will introduce greater flexibility into the system through new statutory management agreements for historic sites.
- We will consult on the scope to reduce uncertainty and ensure early consideration of heritage issues through a greater role for pre-application discussion.
- We will clarify and strengthen protections for World Heritage Sites.
- We will enhance protection for archaeological remains on cultivated land.
- We will provide local planning authorities with new tools to protect locally designated buildings from demolition.

We will improve the heritage protection system by raising the profile of the historic environment, promoting a more joined-up approach, and increasing capacity at local level. To do this:

- We will underpin new legislation with new policy guidance.
- English Heritage will implement a new programme of training, support and capacity-building for English local authorities and local heritage organisations.
- We will improve access to information about the historic environment by introducing a statutory duty for local authorities to maintain or have access to Historic Environment Records.

DCMS, along with Ministers in Wales, Scotland and Northern Ireland, will develop an improved UK-wide system of marine heritage protection that can work effectively alongside national systems. To do this:

- We will broaden the range marine historic assets that can be protected.
- Designation decisions will be made on the basis of special archaeological or historic interest.
- We will make designation decisions easier to understand by publishing new selection criteria for marine designation.
- We will introduce simpler and clearer designation records.
- We will introduce interim protection for marine historic assets.
- We will consider the scope for a new, flexible consents system, including provision for management agreements.
- We will introduce a new statutory duty on the Receiver of Wreck to inform heritage bodies about marine historic assets.

1 Protecting the historic environment in England

1.1 DESIGNATION: WHAT DO WE PROTECT AND HOW?

Summary

We will promote a new holistic approach towards the historic environment by creating a single designation regime that is simple and easy to understand. To do this:

- We will create a single system for national designation to replace listing, scheduling and registering.
- All national designation decisions will be made on the basis of special architectural, historic or archaeological interest.
- We will made designation decisions easier to understand by publishing new detailed selection criteria for national and local designation.
- We will devolve responsibility for national designation to English Heritage.

1. Designation is the first step in an effective heritage protection system. It is a means of identifying those aspects of our past that are most important to us, and explaining why they are important. Effective designation is also the basis for decisions about the way we manage change to the historic environment.

2. An effective heritage protection system needs to strike a balance between protecting what is important and enabling appropriate change. If we fail to provide appropriate protections we will deprive ourselves and future generations of access to our heritage. If we seek to prevent all change, the heritage protection system quickly becomes devalued and unworkable.

3. There is strong public support for protecting our heritage[1]. The designation systems that we have today have been developed over a century and more. They have ensured the protection and preservation of some of our most important and iconic historic assets, and our most treasured landscapes.

4. Despite this public support and proven success, there are frustrations with the current system. Users, including owners, applicants, local planning authorities and community groups, find the number of different designation regimes confusing, slow and inefficient. They find it hard to understand the basis on which designation decisions are made. The practical implications of designation are not always clear[2].

5. We will address these concerns and put designation on a firm footing for the future. For the first time, we will create a single national designation system with a single legislative base. We will make this new system as clear and simple as possible. We will encourage and support greater use of local designation to complement the national system.

What happens now

6. There are currently over half a million nationally designated historic assets in England. Most of these are listed buildings and scheduled ancient monuments, but historic parks and gardens and battlefields are also designated[3].

[1] MORI survey in the *Power of Place* report, Historic Environment Review Steering Group, 2000.

[2] *Review of Heritage Protection: The Way Forward*, DCMS, 2004.

[3] 372,038 entries on the list of buildings, 19,717 Scheduled Ancient Monuments, 9,374 Conservation Areas, 1,587 Registered Historic Parks and Gardens, 59 designated wrecks, 43 registered battlefields and 17 World Heritage Sites (see *Heritage Counts*, English Heritage, 2005 for terrestrial figures).

7. The contribution of the historic environment to the character of our landscape is also recognised in designation regimes administered by the Secretary of State for Environment, Food and Rural Affairs, such as National Parks and Areas of Outstanding Natural Beauty.

8. There is no comprehensive information on the numbers of locally designated assets. There are currently around 10,000 Conservation Areas[4], and around half of all local planning authorities have some list of locally significant buildings[5].

9. Each national designation regime is different. The Secretary of State for Culture, Media and Sport is responsible for designating buildings and ancient monuments. Parks, gardens and battlefields are designated by English Heritage. World Heritage sites are inscribed by UNESCO. At local level, most designation is carried out by local planning authorities (LPAs)[6].

10. It is difficult to obtain a clear picture of the rates of designations. Individual designation regimes have been introduced piecemeal over the last 100 years and the operation of many designation regimes has changed over time. The overall number of designated assets is increasing, but not rapidly[7].

THE NEW SYSTEM

National designation

What can be designated

11. Our current national designation regimes reflect a system that has built up over time. But our understanding of effective heritage protection has moved on, and these traditional distinctions are no longer always helpful. A historic asset may incorporate both above and below ground archaeological remains. Its occupation and use may evolve over time. A more joined-up system is needed that can reflect these changes and enable assets to be managed more effectively.

12. We will promote a new, unified approach to national designation by replacing the current regimes of listing, scheduling and registering with a single, unified system. This system will be used to designate:

- Historic buildings and archaeological sites – incorporating the existing designations of listed buildings and scheduled monuments, and expanded to cover sites of early human activity without structures.
- Historic sites – incorporating the existing designations of registered parks, gardens and battlefields[8].

13. We will clarify the statutory purpose of designation as a means to protect historic assets for current and future generations and provide a framework for managing change.

[4] *Heritage Counts*, English Heritage, 2005. A new study has now been initiated by English Heritage to review these statistics.
[5] *Local Authority Conservation Provision in England*, Oxford Brookes, 2003.
[6] Moveable heritage in the form of museums' collections are designated under a separate system by the Museums, Libraries and Archives Council and are not covered in this White Paper. Similarly, the White Paper does not address other forms of environmental designation (SSSIs, AONBs etc.) or the designations for transport (Register of Historic Vehicles, Register of Historic Vessels etc.).
[7] *Heritage Counts*, English Heritage, 2005.

[8] Although not designated by the new system, World Heritage Sites will also be included on the new Register under 'Historic Sites'.

14. We will further simplify the system by revoking the existing designation of Areas of Archaeological Importance[9]. No new AAIs have been created since 1984, largely because the designation is perceived as being superseded by statutory guidance[10]. We will incorporate the objectives behind AAI designation and the issue of notification of intent to carry out works in new statutory guidance.

Making designation decisions

15. What makes a building, monument or landscape worthy of protection is hard to define. While few would disagree that York Minster should be designated, different people may well give different reasons as to why.

16. Current designation regimes use a range of different criteria to identify what is suitable for protection. Buildings are listed on the basis of "special architectural or historic interest"[11], monuments are selected on the basis of "national importance"[12] and parks and gardens when they are of "special historic interest"[13].

17. As part of the unified system, we will develop a single set of statutory selection criteria for all national designation. The criteria will be as simple as possible, and will be flexible enough to reflect changes in our understanding of the historic environment over time.

18. The concept of 'special interest' used in the listing system has been tested out over many years. It has shown itself to be broad enough to accommodate changing perceptions of the historic environment, and sufficiently neutral to avoid subjective value judgements. In future, all national designation decisions will be made on the basis of 'special architectural, historic or archaeological interest'.

19. While the statutory criteria will remain broad and flexible, we will make the designation system easier to understand by introducing detailed, non-statutory selection criteria. These will be based on the new Principles of Selection[14] that have been issued for listing buildings under the current system. Public consultation has shown that the new criteria, which incorporate broad principles of selection supported by detailed English Heritage selection guides, make the designation process easier to understand. As part of the new national designation system set out in this White Paper, we will develop, consult on and publish new selection criteria for historic buildings and archaeological sites, and historic sites.

Grading

20. Grading helps us to understand the significance of an asset, and informs decisions about management and change. Some current designation systems, notably listing, involve grading, while others, such as scheduling and designation for wrecks, do not.

21. Responses to the 2003 public consultation on the protection of the historic environment showed considerable support for the concept of grading buildings[15]. While there was support for grading in general, many responses suggested

[9] Currently, Canterbury, Chester, Exeter, Hereford and York are designated as Areas of Archaeological Importance.

[10] Mainly PPG15 and PPG16.

[11] Planning (Listed Buildings and Conservation Areas) Act 1990, Section 1(1).

[12] Ancient Monuments and Archaeological Areas Act 1979, Section 1(3).

[13] English Heritage selection criteria, www.english-heritage.org.uk

[14] The general principles have been updated to provide clarity to the listing system to ensure it is transparent and accountable. The statutory criteria and general principles set out the factors taken into account when assessing a building for listing. The revised principles are set out in a planning circular and can be found on the DCMS website at www.culture.gov.uk

[15] 91% of respondents to the Question 4.1, *Review of Heritage Protection: the Way Forward*, DCMS, 2004.

amendments to the system, ranging from clarifying the meanings of current grades, renaming existing grades, or merging grades I and II*[16]. However, there was no clear consensus for change. Our conclusion is that, while their meaning should be clarified, current grades are reasonably well understood by users and should remain.

22. Most nationally designated assets are buildings and are already graded. Under the new, unified system, we will extend the existing grades of GI, GII* and GII to all nationally designated assets. For the time being, all currently scheduled monuments will be classified as GI, but these grades will be reviewed by English Heritage.

Local designation

23. A new national designation regime is only one means of ensuring the effective management and preservation of our heritage. Local designation also has an essential role to play. Local designation provides a means for local communities to identify and to protect the buildings, sites and spaces that matter to them. It helps to build a sense of local identity and distinctiveness, a sense of history, place and belonging.

24. Local planning authorities (LPAs) have a statutory duty to designate Conservation Areas. Conservation Areas are strongly valued by communities and by local planning authorities. As place-based designations, they reflect the joined-up approach to heritage protection that we wish to promote at national level. The current duty on local planning authorities to designate will remain under new legislation.

25. In addition to Conservation Areas, LPAs have the scope to designate individual historic assets. Evidence suggests that more and more authorities are responding to local need and choosing to do so[17]. We support the use of local designation, and want to encourage more authorities to make use of it. As part of our reforms, we will publish new criteria and good practice guidance for local designation, based on the national system, to make it easier for local authorities to develop their own local registers.

Who designates

26. Responsibility for national designation is currently split between the Secretary of State for Culture, Media and Sport and English Heritage. The Secretary of State makes designation decisions, but she is obliged to consider advice from English Heritage[18]. In practice, there are only a very small number of cases where the Secretary of State does not follow the advice of English Heritage in making designation decisions[19].

27. The division between the decision-making role of the Secretary of State and the advisory role of English Heritage is one factor in making designation a lengthy and complex process. To simplify the designation system further, we will transfer statutory responsibility for designation from the Secretary of State for Culture, Media and Sport to English Heritage.

[16] Respectively, 37%, 26% and 17% of respondents to the question, Review of *Heritage Protection: the Way Forward*, DCMS, 2004.

[17] Around half of all LPAs now have some form of local lists, up from 24.2% in 1992/93, and around 20% have other designations, such as 'areas of historic importance'. *The Spirit of Localism*, Joanne Parker, in Context 42, IHBC; *Local Authority conservation Provision in England*, Oxford Brookes, 2003.

[18] As set out in section 1(4) of the Town and Country Planning (Listed Buildings and Conservation Areas) Act 1990, and section 1(3) of the Ancient Monuments and Archaeological Areas Act 1979.

[19] A study of a representative sample of 10% of listing cases from 2002/03 found no cases in which the Secretary of State did not accept the advice of English Heritage.

28. We will balance this transfer of responsibility by introducing new consultation and appeal processes into the system. These are outlined in detail in the next chapter.

29. UNESCO will remain responsible for the inscription of World Heritage Sites. Local Planning Authorities will remain responsible for local designation.

1.2 DESIGNATION: HOW THE SYSTEM WILL WORK

Summary

We will improve designation by involving the public in decisions about what is protected and how, and by making the process simpler and quicker. To do this:

- We will involve the public in shaping a new programme of national designation.
- We will create a new Register of Historic Buildings and Sites of England to replace existing lists and schedules.
- We will introduce simpler and clearer designation records and improve public access to these records through a new internet portal.
- We will open up the system by introducing new consultation and appeal processes.
- We will introduce interim protection for historic assets.
- We will speed up the system and deliver designation decisions faster.

1. National designation involves decisions about which aspects of our heritage we think are most important, and about how this heritage should be protected and managed in the future. These decisions impact on all of us. They affect the places where we live, work and visit.

2. Decisions about designation can be complex and finely balanced. It is right that they are made by highly skilled and experienced professionals. But designation should not be a closed process. Alongside this expert view, there must be an opportunity for those who are affected by these decisions – whether householders, businesses, communities or Government – to make a contribution.

3. Designation places new responsibilities on owners, heritage organisations and Government. Those affected by designation have a right to expect a clear and efficient system. One that clearly explains the process and the basis on which decisions will be taken, and that delivers outcomes quickly.

4. While there is strong public support for designation, people want to see improvements in the current system, and rightly so. There is frustration with the number of separate designation systems, all of which operate in different ways. It can be hard to understand why something has been designated. Information is of variable quality, and can be difficult to access. People feel that there are not enough opportunities for their voice to be heard. Overall, designation systems are seen as slow and cumbersome[20].

5. Our proposals for a new national designation system will address these criticisms. The new system will be open to public participation and scrutiny, and we will initiate a public debate on what we should be seeking to protect in future. It will be a simpler and quicker system, with a single decision-making process, clearer and more accessible information, and faster turnaround times.

What happens now

6. At present, each designation system is recorded and managed separately through the list of buildings ('the List'), the Schedule of Ancient Monuments ('the Schedule'), Registers of Parks, Gardens and Battlefields and the World Heritage list.

[20] *Review of Heritage Protection: the Way Forward*, DCMS, 2004.

7. There is no standard access to information on national designations. Some is provided electronically and is available over the internet, other systems provide only paper records. Designation records themselves are highly variable, ranging from a few sentences for some listed buildings to extensive surveys for some scheduled monuments. Some records include maps and photographs, though the majority do not.

10. Individual designation systems work to varying timescales. On average, listing decisions take around six months from initial application to decision, simple scheduling decisions take approximately two to three months and a complex case around six months, parks and gardens decisions take around two months. The process of inscribing new World Heritage Sites, from appearance on the tentative list to inscription, usually takes a number of years.

11. Designation processes are also different. Some regimes, notably scheduling, involve consultation with owners and local planning authorities. In others, owners are notified only after designation has taken place. In general, opportunities for consultation are limited.

THE NEW SYSTEM

Agreeing national priorities for designation

12. It can be difficult to take decisions about what should be protected in isolation. Informed and balanced choices about what we want to protect need a more planned approach. This enables us to think about those aspects of our heritage that may be under-protected and to decide what may be of special interest. In future, the new designation system will place a stronger emphasis on thematic programmes of protection rather than on individual designation requests.

13. Decisions about what should be protected affect everyone, and it is important that people have an opportunity to have their say. As part of these reforms, English Heritage will carry out a programme of public consultation to develop priorities for a new programme of national designation under the new system.

A single national designation system

14. As part of our new, unified approach, we will create a single system for national designation and improve the information we record about historic assets.

15. The new system will be called the Register of Historic Buildings and Sites of England. It will provide a single point of information about all nationally designated assets in England. It will provide clear and comprehensible information that will improve the way in which we understand, care for and manage our historic assets.

16. Every designated historic asset in England will be recorded in the new Register. The content and format for new Register entries has been tested by English Heritage through a series of pilot projects. The pilots have underlined the crucial role of good information in increasing understanding of a historic asset, in helping owners and managers to feel a sense of ownership and in informing decisions about change[21].

[21] *Heritage Protection Review: Assessment of eight pilot projects for the DCMS*, Historic Environment Conservation, 2006.

17. As a result of these pilot projects, we have developed a format for future designations that will be included on the new Register. Under the new system, every designated asset in England will be recorded using a new Historic Asset Record (HAR). Historic Asset Records will provide enough information to improve understanding and management, but will be short enough to remain workable. Groups of Historic Asset Records that together form a single entity, such as the building and gardens of a historic house, will be linked together using a single Register Entry. To make the system clearer, all new designations will be accompanied by a map. A suggested format for new Register entries is included at Annex 1.

18. The new Register will significantly improve the way in which we record information about our historic assets. It is not intended to provide the last word on significance, but to record what is known at the time of designation. Designation will continue to apply to historic assets as a whole, and local planning authorities will retain their discretion to interpret this significance when determining consents.

Information and access

19. The new Register will provide essential information for those responsible for managing designated historic assets. It will also provide an invaluable new educational resource for both formal and informal learning. We expect the Register to be used not only by regulators, owners and managers, but by anyone with an interest in the historic environment, whether local authorities, heritage organisations, developers, local and national and amenity societies, professional and amateur archaeologists, historians and students.

20. To achieve this, we will ensure easy public access to the new Register by making it available through *The Heritage Gateway*, the new internet portal being developed by English Heritage and partners[22].

Operation of the new system

21. Designation can have a significant impact on the way in which owners manage their property. Owners have a right to expect a process that is clear, open, and that delivers decisions quickly. At the same time, there is a wider community interest in ensuring that the right historic assets are protected in the right way. Designation must be more than just a transaction between regulator and owner. It must ensure sufficient opportunities for all those affected by decisions to contribute their views.

22. The new national designation system will strike a balance between efficiency and openness. It will include new scope for consultation and appeal. It will be easier for people to understand. And it will deliver designation decisions more quickly.

Application

23. We will retain an open system that allows any individual, community or group to nominate a historic asset for protection. To make this application process more efficient, English Heritage will introduce a standard on-line application form for all designation applications.

[22] www.heritagegateway.org.uk/gateway/

Consultation

24. Current designation regimes can be perceived as secretive and unfair. We will open up the new designation system to wide consultation that will provide interested parties with a clear opportunity to contribute their views.

25. Under the new system, owners, LPAs and national amenity societies will be formally consulted on applications to add items to the national Register. Consultees will be asked for their views on how a historic asset matches up against the statutory criteria for designation.

26. In order not to delay the system, consultation will begin as soon as a designation application is received. This will enable representations to be considered alongside research carried out by English Heritage staff.

27. Most designation applications will be subject to these consultation arrangements. The only exceptions will be World Heritage Sites, which are inscribed by UNESCO, and cases rejected by English Heritage at the application stage on the grounds that they do not meet the criteria for designation (approximately a quarter of cases).

Interim protection

28. Opening up the designation system to consultation and scrutiny carries risks. In the past, finding out that their property is under consideration for listing has prompted a small number of owners to damage or demolish a building before it can be listed. While Local Planning Authorities have the ability to serve a Building Preservation Notice (BPNs) to protect buildings they believe to be under immediate threat, they are not often used.

29. Increasing the amount of consultation in the process increases the risk of pre-emptive damage. To address this, the new system will introduce interim protection for historic assets under consideration for designation. This protection will begin from the point of public consultation on an application to designate and will protect the asset as if it were designated. Interim protection will replace the current system of BPNs.

30. Interim protection will not apply to World Heritage Sites, which are inscribed by UNESCO, or to cases rejected by English Heritage at the application stage on the grounds that they do not meet the criteria for designation.

31. Interim protection will last until the end of the designation process. If English Heritage decides not to designate the asset, interim protection will continue to apply until the end of the period in which an appeal against the decision can be made. If an appeal is launched, interim protection will remain in place until a final decision has been made.

Appeals

32. The new designation system will be clear and open, with new opportunities for consultation. But we acknowledge that there will always be a small number of contentious cases. As part of the new system, we will introduce a right of appeal to the Secretary of State for Culture, Media and Sport on designation decisions made by English Heritage.

33. Appeals will be open to those with an interest in a historic asset, including owners, consultees, applicants and local planning authorities. Appeals will be possible where those with an

interest are unhappy with the outcome of a designation decision and may be made on the grounds that relevant material has not been taken into account or irrelevant material has been considered; that the evidence has not been assessed appropriately; or in cases of factual error (e.g. the wrong building has been designated).

34. Appellants will have 28 days to appeal against English Heritage decisions. Appeals to the Secretary of State will be considered by a new independent panel, who will recommend whether English Heritage's decision should be upheld or a new decision made. To consider appeals, the Secretary of State will either select a panel member with expertise in the particular type of asset under consideration, or ask for recommendations to be made by the panel as a whole.

35. The appeals system will not apply to interim protection and will not apply to World Heritage Sites, which are inscribed by UNESCO, or to cases rejected by English Heritage at the application stage on the grounds that they do not meet the criteria for designation.

A faster system

36. We recognise that designation has, in the past, been a slow and frustrating process. Bringing together all national designation under a single process administered by a single organisation will enable us to create a more efficient system. Under the new designation system, decisions will be delivered faster. English Heritage will agree new performance targets for designation with the Secretary of State, and will publish their performance against these targets.

Transition to the new system

37. The new system outlined in this White Paper will be used for all newly designated assets. But there remains a legacy of around half a million existing designation records, mainly listed buildings.

38. Almost all items designated under existing regimes will continue to be protected under new legislation[23]. The focus for the future will be on working with the public and the sector to identify future themes for designation and on implementing the new system rather than on reviewing all existing designations.

[23] The only exception to this will be Areas of Archaeological Importance (AAIs) which will be revoked as a specific designation.

1.3 HERITAGE PROTECTION AND PLANNING

Summary

We will support sustainable communities by putting the historic environment at the heart of an effective planning system. To do this:

- We will streamline regulation by merging Listed Building Consent and Scheduled Monument Consent, and by consulting on the merging of Conservation Area Consent with planning permission.
- We will introduce greater flexibility into the system through new statutory management agreements for historic sites.
- We will consult on the scope to reduce uncertainty and ensure early consideration of heritage issues through a greater role for pre-application discussion.
- We will clarify and strengthen protections for World Heritage Sites.
- We will enhance protection for archaeological remains on cultivated land.
- We will provide local planning authorities with new tools to protect locally designated buildings from demolition.

1. The planning system in England is in the process of radical reform. The Government's vision is for sustainable communities – places where people want to live and work, now and in the future – delivered through a planning system that ensures greater speed, efficiency and certainty while maintaining wide community participation.

2. Heritage has a crucial role to play in delivering sustainable communities. For many people, it is heritage that provides their community with a sense of character, distinctiveness and identity and makes it somewhere they want to live. In towns and cities, heritage has provided the starting point for imaginative and successful regeneration. In the countryside it plays an important role in rural regeneration. As pressures on the planning system grow, it is often heritage that provides a focal point for engaging communities in decisions about preservation and development.

3. Protecting heritage is an integral part of the planning system[24]. In recent years, the sector has responded well to wider planning reforms. English Heritage have reformed their advisory services to deliver a quicker and more effective service[25]; we have improved the evidence base to make a convincing case for the role of heritage in regeneration[26]; and we have highlighted how historic assets can provide prime examples of sustainable development.

4. But these changes, though important, have been incremental. Research and consultation has confirmed that there is the potential, and the appetite, for much more significant reform. Reform that simplifies the system, streamlines and rationalises regulation, and reduces the burdens on users and on local authorities, while continuing to provide appropriate levels of protection[27].

[24] 30% of planning decisions have heritage implications (*Heritage Under Pressure*, English Heritage, 2002). In 2005/06 33,500 applications for Listed Building Consent, 951 applications for Scheduled Monument Consent and 3,400 applications for Conservation Area Consent were decided (*Heritage Counts*, English Heritage, 2006).

[25] Memorandum submitted by English Heritage to the Culture, Media and Sport Select Committee, 2006.

[26] See, for example, *Heritage Dividend*, English Heritage, 2002; *Regeneration and the Historic Environment – heritage as a catalyst for better social and economic regeneration*, English Heritage, 2005; *Heritage Works – The use of historic buildings in regeneration*, RICS, BPF, EH, Drivers Jonas, 2006.

[27] *Unification of Consent Regimes*, ODPM, 2004; *Householder Development Consents Review – Steering Group Report*, DCLG, 2006; *Barker Review of Land Use Planning*, TSO, 2006; *Consent Regimes – Reducing Unnecessary Bureaucracy*, ODPM and Cabinet Office, 2006.

5. A new challenge has been set by the recent Barker Review[28], which has urged the Government to go further with planning reform to create a more flexible, responsive and efficient planning system that can support economic growth and productivity.

6. We will respond to these challenges by reforming heritage protection within the planning system. We will streamline the system by bringing together consent regimes where we can. We will reduce burdens by introducing new flexible management tools. We will consult on ways to improve certainty for developers and ensure early and effective consideration of heritage issues in large-scale planning applications. And we will enhance protections for some types of historic asset. This package of reforms will reshape the heritage protection system to meet the vision set out in the Barker report and being delivered by the forthcoming Planning Reform White Paper.

The new system

Streamlining regulation

7. We recognise that the current system of heritage consents can be time-consuming and bureaucratic, particularly when dealing with complex sites which include a number of different designations. Numerous studies have suggested that there is scope for greater integration of consent regimes within the planning system[29]. The consensus is that integration should be gradual and taken forward on a case-by-case basis rather than in a single step.

8. With this in mind, we have considered the scope for streamlining current heritage consent regimes. For the time being, we think there continues to be a case for some distinct heritage controls, separate from planning permission, but that in other cases, unification may be appropriate. The reforms set out in this White Paper may provide a stepping stone for the further rationalisation of consent regimes in future as recommended in the Barker Review.

Listed Building Consent and Scheduled Monument Consent

9. We will streamline the heritage consent regime by removing the current systems of Listed Building Consent and Scheduled Monument Consent and replacing them with a new, unified consent for Registered Buildings and Archaeological Sites called Historic Asset Consent.

10. The legislative base underpinning the new consent will be aligned. Detailed legislative change will be consulted on in advance of new legislation, but likely key changes are set out in Annex 2.

11. Local planning authorities will be responsible for determining Historic Asset Consent, with involvement from the Secretary of State for Communities and Local Government and from English Heritage as appropriate.

12. Appeals against decisions relating to Historic Asset Consent will be made to the Secretary of State for Communities and Local Government and appeals heard by the Planning Inspectorate.

13. Registered Historic Sites[30] will continue to be managed through the planning system.

[28] *Barker Review of Land Use Planning*, TSO, 2006.

[29] *Barker Review of Land Use Planning*, TSO, 2006; *Unification of Consent Regimes*, ODPM, 2004; *Householder Development Consents Review – Steering Group Report*, DCLG, 2006.

[30] Currently Registered parks, gardens and battlefields, and World Heritage Sites.

Conservation Area Consent

14. Alongside the new unified heritage consent, we have considered the scope for further streamlining the consent regime.

15. At present, total or significant demolition in a conservation area requires Conservation Area Consent. We propose that Conservation Area Consent should be abolished as a separate consent process and merged with planning permission.

16. A merger along these lines would not reduce levels of protection for Conservation Areas. We would ensure that heritage considerations would be given sufficient weight in the planning process by making it clear in statutory guidance that conservation professionals should be involved in considering planning applications for sites within a conservation area and in any pre-application discussions. This would complement any policies relating to Conservation Areas in Local Development Frameworks.

17. While it would not reduce protection, this proposal would mean that development that currently requires both planning permission and Conservation Area Consent would only require one application.

18. While we are broadly satisfied that the level of protection provided under this proposal is appropriate, we are keen to address the issues arising out of the Shimizu judgement[31] which means that partial demolition of an unlisted building in a Conservation Area no longer requires Conservation Area Consent. A merger of Conservation Area Consent with planning permission would be an opportunity to raise levels of protection back to pre-Shimizu levels, so that full or partial demolition of an unlisted building in a Conservation Area would require planning permission.

19. While Conservation Area Consent would be removed as a separate consent process, the power to designate Conservation Areas would not be affected.

20. We recognise that this is a new proposal and wish to give people who have an interest an opportunity to contribute their views. We are therefore consulting formally on the proposal. Details of how to respond are set out in Part 4.

The Ecclesiastical Exemption

21. A unified designation and consent system will impact on the operation of the Ecclesiastical Exemption from Listed Building Consent.

22. Listed places of worship are some of our most valuable historic assets, and make up a significant proportion of Grade I listed buildings. The Ecclesiastical Exemption provides a mechanism for denominations to operate their own systems of internal control for works to listed buildings, subject to certain safeguards. The Government supports the principle of the Exemption, which reduces burdens on the planning system while maintaining protection, and which reflects the particular need of historic assets in use as places of worship.

23. The Ecclesiastical Exemption will continue under the new system. Register entries relating to ecclesiastical assets in use as places of worship (such as parish churches together with their attached churchyards and any separately designated tombs) will be exempt from Historic Asset Consent. The Exemption will not be extended to other ecclesiastical assets or to other denominations. Ecclesiastical buildings will remain fully subject to planning control.

[31] Shimizu (UK) Limited v Westminster City Council in 1997.

24. In advance of any legislation, we will work with the exempt denominations to agree the operation of the Exemption under the new system, on the understanding that denominational systems should provide similar levels of consultation and engagement to secular systems of control.

Introducing greater flexibility

Heritage Partnership Agreements

25. For owners and managers of complex assets, the current heritage consent system can be time consuming and burdensome. Owners may need to make a large number of consent applications, often for routine or repetitive works[32]. It can be unclear what works will need consent and what will not. As well as the direct costs of making and managing an application, repeated applications may delay wider development.

26. Management agreements can offer a solution to the challenge of managing complex historic assets. Research[33] has shown that they can:

- improve partnerships and dialogue between stakeholders;
- improve understanding of a historic site, especially among non-heritage professionals;
- help owners and managers to clarify their future plans for the management of sites;
- encourage a positive approach to medium and long-term management which can prevent drastic and costly repairs later on;
- reduce the number of unnecessary consent applications by providing more certainty and clarity on which works may or may not require consent; and
- substantially reduce numbers of individual consents.

27. Management agreements have been used in the past, both for listed buildings and scheduled ancient monuments, but often have lacked statutory force. As part of a new heritage protection system, we will therefore bring forward statutory provision for management agreements, called Heritage Partnership Agreements (HPAs), by enabling local planning authorities to provide advance consent for works.

Operation of Agreements

28. Heritage Partnership Agreements are likely to be of most benefit for large complex sites under single ownership and with many similar types of asset, such as bridges on a road network, London Underground stations, or on large landholdings with multiple historic and nature conservation assets.

29. Heritage Partnership Agreements are only likely to succeed where owners and local planning authorities have a strong commitment to a site. Agreements will therefore be a voluntary option for both owners and authorities.

30. The core stakeholders involved in an HPA will be the owners and managers of a site, the local planning authority and, where appropriate, English Heritage. Statutory consultation on HPAs will match the statutory consultation arrangements for Historic Asset Consent, and Agreements will be subject to regular monitoring and review involving partners and consultees. Circumstances such as a change in ownership, or a major development, will trigger a review of Agreements.

[32] *Heritage Protection Review: Assessment of eight pilot projects for the DCMS*, Historic Environment Conservation, 2006.

[33] *Heritage Protection Review: Assessment of eight pilot projects for the DCMS*, Historic Environment Conservation, 2006; *Streamlining Listed Building Consent: Lessons from the use of management agreements*, ODPM and EH, 2003.

31. If, during the course of monitoring, it is found there has been a breach of the HPA, partners will need to review the Agreement and consider whether to proceed and whether any enforcement action should follow. If there have been breaches that are outside the statutory consent system, partners may need to consider if there is sufficient commitment to continue. In the event of more serious breaches, the site owner will be acting outside the Agreement and within the normal consent system. Enforcement of these breaches would lie within the normal heritage consent system.

32. Heritage Partnership Agreements can take considerable time and resources to develop and agree[34]. Agreements will need a life span sufficient to deliver the efficiencies that will justify this investment. It is intended that Agreements should run for a minimum of five years, with the option of extension to 10 years by mutual agreement.

33. All works carried out under a Heritage Partnership Agreement will be recorded by the site owner or manager and local planning authorities will be notified.

34. Large-scale HPAs that cross authority boundaries will be negotiated by English Heritage.

Content of Agreements

35. HPAs will need to be flexible documents to accommodate a range of different types of sites. Experience from piloting the Agreements suggests that in general they should include three parts:

- Administrative information, including information about the parties involved in the HPA and their role; the Register entry and map for the site; practicalities of the Agreement, including an agreed timeframe for the HPA, a method of monitoring, review and renewal, an agreed grievance procedure etc.
- An overarching conservation framework for the site that can act as the context for any decisions about particular works, and assist in preparing any detailed consent applications. Many sites will already have a conservation framework in place (for example as part of a World Heritage Site management plan or as part of an environmental stewardship scheme). The HPA would work within such existing agreements, and within the approach to managing the historic environment set out in local authority local plan policies.
- Specified works, which may take two forms: an agreement of works that are agreed not to require consent; and works that would otherwise be covered by the new heritage consent but have been pre-agreed with a specification outlining the materials and methods to be used.

36. Not all works affecting historic assets will be suitable for pre-agreement through a Heritage Partnership Agreement. Major interventions involving significant change will be better handled as part of the specific consent regime, where detailed consideration of particular plans can be considered.

Next steps

37. In advance of new legislation, English Heritage will produce new guidance for owners, local planning authorities and other interested parties in developing and managing Heritage Partnership Agreements.

[34] Agreements developed as part of English Heritage pilots took between one and five weeks to develop, excluding time for consultation. *Heritage Protection Review: Assessment of eight pilot projects for the DCMS*, Historic Environment Conservation, 2006.

Reducing uncertainty

38. Most designation decisions are straightforward and uncontroversial. They are supported by owners, by local planning authorities and by local communities, who recognise and value the importance of heritage protection.

39. In a minority of cases, however, designation can be a highly contested and controversial process. People can and do disagree about whether a particular building or site merits protection. Problems can be particularly acute when designation is being considered at the same time as development proposals for a site.

40. Designation is, and will continue to be, a stand-alone decision based on the intrinsic interest of a building or site rather than on wider planning criteria. This enables decisions about designation to be taken on their merits rather than in response to short-term pressure. It is the right approach for a heritage protection system that seeks to secure the long-term future of our historic assets. But it does mean that in a small number of cases, designation can delay, derail or prevent development. This has been highlighted as a particular problem in the case of large-scale planning applications, where advanced proposals for major developments can be substantially delayed by listing.

41. The changes outlined in this White Paper will help to reduce the scope for conflict in the heritage protection system. Designation decisions will be taken faster. They will be based on clear and understandable criteria that have been subject to wide public consultation. Interested parties are more likely to be aware of potential designations, and there will be opportunities to have decisions formally reviewed.

42. While these changes will lead to substantial improvements in the system, we are considering whether there is scope to go further, particularly in relation to large-scale developments. Ongoing planning reforms have highlighted the valuable role of pre-application discussions in improving the quality of planning decisions and providing greater certainty for developers in the planning process. The recent Barker Review has challenged Government to expand this approach further.

43. The current heritage protection system makes extensive use of pre-application assessment and discussion in relation to archaeology[35]. This approach has proved useful in enabling development to take place while mitigating its effects on important archaeological remains[36]. As part of reforming the heritage protection system, we will consider whether this pre-application approach should be extended to embrace all historic assets likely to be affected by major developments.

44. At the same time, Government strongly supports the use of Certificates of Immunity as a means of providing developers with certainty that a building will not be listed. Under the new system, we propose expanding the scope of these Certificates, so that applications may be made at any time, not only once a planning application has been submitted. We also propose expanding the scope of COIs, so that they may encompass entire sites rather than individual historic assets.

[35] As set out in *Planning Policy Guidance 16: Archaeology and Planning*, DoE, 1990.

[36] Memorandum submitted by the Archaeology Forum to the Culture, Media and Sport Select Committee, 2006.

45. Taken together, we feel that these two changes would provide developers with greater certainty when considering or preparing planning applications for major developments that might affect historic assets. These are new proposals and they require further consideration. As a next step, we are inviting those with an interest to contribute their views. Details on how to respond are set out in Chapter 4.

Enhancing protection

46. Our proposals are aimed at ensuring that the heritage protection system can work effectively as part of a simpler and more efficient planning system. But we recognise that in some cases, the current system may not be working effectively to safeguard our historic assets, and there is a case for increasing levels of protection.

Class Consents

47. The Class Consents system exempts certain types of activity from Scheduled Monument Consent by providing a blanket consent[37]. We strongly support the principle of Class Consents as a means of reducing regulatory burdens and streamlining the operation of the heritage protection system.

48. While the system works well in most cases, there is evidence to show that the process does not provide appropriate protection in a limited number of cases. Class Consent No 1 applies to agricultural cultivation and to horticulture. For agricultural cultivation, the Consent permits 'same depth' cultivation to be carried out on scheduled sites previously lawfully cultivated. It was implemented on the basis that continuous same depth ploughing does no archaeological damage. Research carried out by the Department for Environment, Food and Rural Affairs (DEFRA) and English Heritage[38] has shown that this is not the case, and that such cultivation causes damage to a significant number of scheduled ancient monuments[39].

49. Given the evidence of damage to nationally important monuments, we will revoke the section of Class Consent No 1 relating to agriculture. We recognise that it would be an unreasonable burden for landowners to take large areas of land entirely out of cultivation. Nor is there the evidence base to justify this approach. Instead, we will reform the current system based on a management agreement approach that makes use of existing schemes where possible.

50. Where a historic asset is managed appropriately through an Environmental Stewardship Scheme, Historic Asset Consent (HAC) will not be required[40]. Where there is no appropriate Environmental Stewardship Scheme, a Heritage Partnership Agreement may be negotiated to manage the site. HPAs relating to monuments under cultivation will be negotiated between the site owner, the local planning authority and English Heritage and will be designed to last for 10 years. Policy guidance will make clear that

[37] The Class Consents cover Agricultural, Horticultural and Forestry Works, Works by British Coal Corporation or their licensees, Works by British Waterways Board, Works for the Repair or Maintenance of Machinery, Works urgently necessary for safety or health, Works by the Commission, Works of Archaeological Evaluation, Works carried out under certain agreements concerning ancient monuments, Works grant aided under Section 24 of the Act, and Works undertaken by the Royal Commission on the Historical Monuments of England or the Royal Commission on Ancient and Historical Monuments of Wales.

[38] Conservation of Scheduled Monuments in Cultivation (COSMIC) project, EH and DEFRA.

[39] The COSMIC study assessed the risk of 'same depth' cultivation to 159 scheduled and unscheduled monuments in the East Midlands. Of these, 39% were deemed to be at serious risk from cultivation, 31% at high risk and 9% at moderate risk. The study demonstrated that 66% of land managers underestimated the depth to which their cultivation operations were disturbing sites.

[40] Any of the entry level or organic entry level schemes relating to historic and landscape features, or any of the higher level scheme historic environment options, will remove the need for separate HAC.

the objective of any HPAs relating to historic assets under cultivation will be to enable continued cultivation wherever possible.

51. We recognise that it will take time to negotiate management agreements for historic assets under cultivation. The section of Class Consent No 1 relating to agriculture will therefore remain in force until such time as a HPA is proposed by either the local planning authority or by English Heritage.

World Heritage Sites

52. World Heritage Sites are internationally recognised as having outstanding universal value. The reforms outlined in this White Paper will, for the first time, provide a clear framework for the way in which WHSs operate alongside other elements of the heritage protection system. This Review has also provided the opportunity to consider whether any additional protections are required. Our view is that, while in general WHSs are adequately protected, there is a case for some small changes that will clarify and, in some cases strengthen, current protections.

53. As part of the reforms in this White Paper, we will put in place two new measures to clarify and strengthen the protection afforded to World Heritage Sites. First, as part of a wider review of the Call-in Directions, we intend to introduce specific notification and call-in requirements for significant development affecting World Heritage Sites. Second, we will update planning policy to strengthen the consideration of World Heritage Sites within the planning system.

54. In advance of legislative change, we have taken into account concerns of UNESCO and others about current levels of protection. We will therefore issue a planning circular which will further recognise in national policy the need to protect World Heritage Sites as sites of outstanding universal value, and will make more prominent the need to create a management plan for each WHS, including, where needed, the delineation of a buffer zone around it. This update will also be an opportunity to clarify the impact of some recent planning reforms, such as the introduction of Design and Access Statements, in relation to World Heritage Sites.

55. We will also include World Heritage Sites as Article 1(5) land under the Town and Country Planning (General Permitted Development) Order 1995. This would put them on the same footing as other protected areas such as conservation areas, National Parks and Areas of Outstanding Natural Beauty, where permitted development rights are more restricted, not being available for minor changes such as artificial stone cladding or dormer windows. Such changes might be on a relatively small scale but in some circumstances – and particularly on a cumulative basis – could have a significant effect in terms of loss of protection in sensitive areas.

Protection for local designations

56. National designation, and the associated consent regimes, are only one aspect of managing change to historic assets. We encourage the use of local designation to provide communities with the opportunity to identify and manage those aspects of their heritage that are important to them.

57. Almost half of all local planning authorities already produce some sort of list of locally significant buildings or sites, and we expect the use of local lists to increase over time.

58. At present, local authorities have a number of options available to them to provide additional protection for their local designations. The inclusion of a historic asset on a local list can be a material consideration within the planning system. This can be further strengthened by placing local lists on the relevant Historic Environment Record or reflecting the local list in local plan policies[41]. In addition, local authorities may restrict works to locally listed buildings permitted under the General Permitted Development Order by making an Article 4(1) Direction limiting permitted development rights.

59. In general, we are satisfied that there are adequate means of providing protection for locally designated assets through effective use of the planning system. We will encourage local planning authorities to make greater use of these existing mechanisms by reflecting the importance of local designation, and outlining the protections available, in new statutory guidance.

60. At the same time, we will strengthen the protection against demolition for locally designated buildings. We will do this by making the demolition of all locally designated buildings 'development' and by granting permitted development rights for demolition, leaving local planning authorities with the option of making an Article 4(1) direction to remove these rights where appropriate.

[41] Fewer than half of the local authorities keeping lists of locally valued or designated buildings support these through specific policies within their development plan – Atkins summary report. Research carried out by Peter Boland in 1997/98 found that of 20 appeal decisions relating to buildings on local lists, only one was negative as regards a local list building, leading him to conclude that "Appeal Inspectors appear highly accepting of Local Lists, viewing them as a perfectly proper exercise of the powers of local planning authorities".

1.4 HISTORIC ENVIRONMENT SERVICES AT LOCAL LEVEL

Summary

We will improve the heritage protection system by raising the profile of the historic environment, promoting a more joined-up approach, and increasing capacity at local level. To do this:

- We will underpin new legislation with new policy guidance from English Heritage.
- English Heritage will implement a new programme of training, support and capacity-building for local authorities and local heritage organisations.
- We will improve access to information about the local historic environment by introducing a statutory duty on local authorities to maintain or have access to a Historic Environment Record.

1. The historic environment contributes to a broad range of local priorities. Local heritage can underpin sustainable communities, drive regeneration and tourism, and support sustainable development. It is a vast and valuable educational resource for both formal and informal learning. And it has its own intrinsic value as an expression of our past and of our identity.

2. The complex role of heritage is reflected in the varied configuration of historic environment services at local level. There is no single model for historic environment services. Their size, location, strength and specialisms vary from authority to authority. Reflecting this diversity, heritage professionals need to be highly skilled specialists, capable of working across disciplinary silos and able to contribute to planning, to regeneration, to urban design, to rural development, to community cohesion and to education agendas[42 & 43].

3. The importance of heritage to such a diverse range of local authority priorities is a strength, but it can also have drawbacks. Because it contributes to so many different agendas, the historic environment can lack a clear lead within local authorities. The range and complexity of the issues involved, together with the non-statutory nature of most services, can leave local authorities unsure as to where best they should focus attention and resources.

4. Complementing the role of local authorities, the local historic environment inspires huge numbers of volunteers[44]. The heritage protection system relies on the commitment of voluntary organisations such as the National Amenity Societies and of thousands of local historical and special interest groups. These organisations contribute essential expertise and knowledge to the process, supported at national level by enabling organisations such as Planning Aid and Heritage Link.

5. The reforms set out in this White Paper will lead to changes in the way in which local planning authorities and voluntary and community sector organisations operate. Delivering a new heritage protection system will involve:

- a clearer and more effective role for authorities, individuals, communities and voluntary sector organisations in national designation;

[42] Most conservation specialists are located within planning teams, but often as part of a specialist team. Archaeological specialists can be based in planning departments, the museum service, environment or community learning. Heritage specialists may also be architects, town planners, design or regeneration specialists.

[43] The number of historic environment professionals employed by local authorities is variable. The most recent large-scale surveys suggest an upward trend in the numbers of archaeologists in recent years, and static levels of conservation specialists, though anecdotal evidence suggests that numbers are declining in some areas.

[44] The most recent *Taking Part* survey, 2005/06, estimates that about 1.1% of the adult population in England (equivalent to 400,000 adults) were involved in heritage volunteering in 2005/06.

- a renewed role for local designation as a means of encouraging local communities to identify and manage aspects of their local heritage;
- a greater emphasis on heritage issues in wider planning and land management processes;
- negotiating and operating new Heritage Partnership Agreements where appropriate; and
- a unified consents system, incorporating advice from English Heritage and other consultees where needed.

6. These changes build on and complement many of the reforms that are already taking place within professions, voluntary sector organisations and local authorities. They will encourage local authorities to develop a greater sense of ownership of the local historic environment, and provide new opportunities to increase community engagement.

7. To support local authorities and voluntary and community organisations to operate the new system, we will provide local authorities with better guidance on central Government priorities, we will improve the training, capacity building and support available to authorities and the voluntary sector, and we will improve access to information on the historic environment at local level.

Providing a clear policy framework

8. While the historic environment is reflected in statutory guidance, and in some local authority performance indicators, some authorities have indicated that they are unclear what their priorities should be[45]. This lack of clarity is partly historic, reflecting traditional distinctions between historic environment professionals, and partly a reflection of the sheer variety and scope of the historic environment. A clear statement about the role of local authority historic environment services will help to improve understanding of the multiple roles of the heritage protection system and to raise the profile and status of historic environment services.

9. This White Paper provides the first step towards simplifying and clarifying the heritage protection system. As a next step, English Heritage will build on this White Paper by publishing new guidance on the outcomes local authorities should be seeking from their historic environment services. This guidance will be underpinned by the forthcoming new English Heritage Conservation Principles that will set a clear conservation philosophy to guide approaches to managing the historic environment, and by standards and guidance published by the professional bodies.

10. We hope that the combination of this White Paper, the new English Heritage guidance, the Conservation Principles, and advice from the professional bodies on accreditation, will enable and encourage local planning authorities to develop a clear vision for how they would like to develop their historic environment services in future.

[45] *Historic Environment Local Delivery Project*, Atkins, 2006.

Improving capacity

11. Effective management of the historic environment at local level requires the right skills, knowledge and understanding, not only for heritage specialists, but in all areas where decision-making has an impact on heritage.

12. In recognition of this, English Heritage have created the Historic Environment Local Management (HELM) programme, a website and training initiative designed to build capacity within local authorities. At the same time, DCMS and DCLG have encouraged local authorities to appoint Historic Environment Champions, in most cases from among their elected members. Since 2004, over half of all local authorities have appointed champions, and numbers continue to increase[46].

13. While HELM and the Champions initiative have had a positive impact, the reforms set out in this White Paper present a new challenge. Delivering the new heritage protection system will require new skills and knowledge at local level. Local planning authorities will need to develop:

- greater cross-disciplinary skills development and working between buildings professionals and archaeologists that can complement existing cross-disciplinary working on issues such as community involvement, regeneration, education and town planning;
- improved understanding of historic environment issues across a broader professional spectrum to ensure that heritage issues are considered as part of wider policy and practice; and
- greater cross-border and cross-tier working, with greater use of service level agreements and more information sharing between professionals.

14. These skills requirements are not new concepts. Much of the training and capacity building work being developed by the Academy for Sustainable Communities in response to the Egan Review, through the HELM programme, and by professional institutes and heritage organisations, is designed to achieve similar aims. We wish to build on the progress that has already been made, and encourage all local authorities to come up to the standards of the best.

15. To help achieve this, we will implement a step-change in the advice and support provided to local authorities by building on the current HELM programme. English Heritage, working with the professional bodies, will roll out new training to all local authority historic environment staff and Historic Environment Champions, and to most other non-heritage staff with an interest in the historic environment, and most elected members. New training will also be made available to wider organisations, including amenity societies, regional bodies, and other agencies to enable them to contribute fully to the new system.

Improving information

16. Improved access to clear, comprehensive and current information about the historic environment will underpin operation of the new heritage protection system. It will help to inform timely decision-making by owners, developers and local planning authorities, and will guide the engagement of voluntary sector organisations. It will also help individuals and communities to gain a better understanding of their local environment and play an active role in decisions about its future.

[46] English Heritage is working towards a target of HE champions in 75% of local authorities by April 2008.

17. Despite the impetus provided by e-planning, many local authorities continue to maintain heritage information in a variety of standalone systems and to variable standards.

18. The most established source of information, particularly for archaeological sites, is the national 'network' of 85 historic environment records (HERs) maintained on a discretionary basis by county councils and unitary authorities[47]. However, few HERs are currently accessible over the Internet or provide comprehensive coverage of historic buildings.

19. To encourage a more joined-up approach to information management that can meet the needs of all stakeholders in the new system, we will secure existing provision by creating a new statutory duty for local authorities to maintain or have access to a HER. We will encourage and support the development of HERs as more comprehensive and accessible sources of heritage information. And we will seek to embed the historic environment more firmly within wider e-government delivery programmes, particularly e-planning.

Statutory Historic Environment Records

20. Statutory HERs will have a central role in enabling the delivery of a new heritage protection system. Their main purpose will be to inform the management of the historic environment to support sustainable development, both within the planning system and through other management systems such as environmental stewardship schemes.

21. Alongside this, HERs will continue to contribute to our understanding and enjoyment of the historic environment by providing a resource for local history, conservation, education and tourism projects and linking to services offered by museums, archives and libraries.

22. To fulfil these roles, each HER will need :

- databases which provide a comprehensive, up-to-date local record of the historic environment and an index to related information sources;
- a linked GIS to help analyse and present this information alongside other environmental datasets (such as characterisation studies); and
- skilled curatorial staff who can communicate with diverse audiences, including LPA staff, householders, developers and community groups.

23. If they are to be used effectively, the content of HERs will need to be made as accessible as possible, including through the Planning Portal and Heritage Gateway. Their reference collections (which may include copies of relevant photographs, plans, surveys, reports, articles and maps) will also need to be available for public consultation.

24. English Heritage will support local planning authorities to develop and improve their HERs through new training and capacity building, and through new national standards and guidance. The new training and guidance will help to establish a new perception of HERs as an integral part of the information systems used by all historic environment professionals at local level.

[47] English Heritage maintains a HER on behalf of London Borough Councils. Some district councils and national park authorities also maintain their own HER.

2 Protecting the historic environment in Wales

The Welsh Assembly Government will develop a simpler, more efficient and more responsive heritage protection system in Wales. To do this:

DESIGNATION

- We will consult on revised designation criteria for national designation and develop detailed selection guides to support them.
- We will extend formal consultation with owners and others ahead of designation.
- We will provide a statutory right of appeal against designation decisions and introduce new arrangements for independent appeal.
- We will set up a unified statutory Register of Historic Sites and Buildings of Wales, including listed buildings, scheduled monuments and registered parks and gardens.
- We will end dual designation (listing and scheduling) for historic assets.

THE PLANNING SYSTEM

- We will bring the demolition of locally designated buildings within development control.
- We will introduce statutory consultation with Cadw, the Garden History Society and the Welsh Historic Gardens Trust in respect of planning applications affecting registered parks and gardens and their settings.
- We will broaden and develop existing work in the area of urban and rural landscape characterisation.
- We will strengthen protection and provide more planning policy guidance for World Heritage Sites.
- We will review the current scope of the Ecclesiastical Exemption and planned changes with the exempt denominations.

ACCESS TO INFORMATION

- We will introduce a requirement on local authorities to adopt and support historic environment records either directly or through the agency of others.

Introduction

1. Wales has a rich historic environment with a wealth of well-preserved prehistoric sites and famous Roman sites. The iconic castles of the Welsh Princes and of Edward I are celebrated and appreciated by many visitors from the UK and abroad. Other structures have a special resonance in Wales and are closely associated with Welsh identity, including the industrial archaeology and terraced housing of the south Wales valleys, the chapels of Wales and small vernacular dwellings as found especially in the north and west.

2. Protection of the historic environment of Wales is a key priority for the Welsh Assembly Government. Its strategic planning framework, *Planning Policy Wales*, emphasises the importance of protecting Wales' historic environment in its diverse forms – archaeology and ancient monuments, listed buildings, conservation areas and historic parks, gardens and landscapes. The historic environment can contribute significantly to the Assembly Government's wider strategic objectives, as set out in *Wales: A Better Country*, the Wales Spatial and Environment Strategy. It can help generate environmental and economic benefits, aid sustainability, enhance skills, strengthen Wales' cultural identity and support lifelong learning and community development.

3. The distinctive nature of the historic environment in Wales, together with different systems and practice, means that, in some circumstances, a different approach is required from that adopted in England. The main elements, aims and objectives of this White Paper apply equally to Wales and are not referred to in this section. But there are some areas where different arrangements for Wales will be necessary to suit Welsh circumstances.

The legislative framework in Wales

4. Statutory responsibility for heritage protection in Wales rests with the National Assembly for Wales and is administered by Cadw, the division within the Welsh Assembly Government with responsibility for protecting, conserving and promoting the historic environment of Wales. From May 2007, with the implementation of the Government of Wales Act 2006, this statutory responsibility will rest with the Welsh Assembly Government.

5. Currently, primary legislation relating to the historic environment is shared with England. In any new England and Wales Heritage Protection Bill, in line with the new arrangements brought into force by the Government of Wales Act 2006, we would propose to seek equivalent powers for Welsh Ministers as would be given to English Ministers, including the making of subordinate legislation. We would also propose to seek powers for the National Assembly for Wales to pass Assembly Measures. This would give the National Assembly enhanced legislative competence in relation to specific devolved matters in aspects of the historic environment.

The heritage protection system in Wales

6. Though it shares the same primary legislation with England, important elements of the heritage protection system are managed differently in Wales.

7. There are around 30,000 listed buildings, 4,000 scheduled ancient monuments, 372 Registered Parks and Gardens and 2 World Heritage Sites in Wales, with a further site nominated for such status. Almost all listed buildings have detailed list descriptions. Notification of owners of intention to list has already been introduced. A programme to enhance the scheduling of the better known archaeological site types is underway and will be largely completed by 2010. New scheduling descriptions are detailed, include site maps and consultation is standard practice. In partnership with the Countryside Council for Wales and ICOMOS UK, Cadw has compiled a Landscapes Register which includes 36 'outstanding' and 22 'special' historic landscapes. There is currently no Battlefields Register in Wales but Cadw, in partnership with the Royal Commission on the Ancient and Historical Monuments of Wales, is looking into the feasibility of introducing one.

8. The four Welsh Archaeological Trusts provide a comprehensive regional archaeological service in Wales. They maintain the regional Historic Environment Records, provide heritage management and development control advice to the unitary authorities and national parks in their regions, and to many other organisations. They also undertake a wider range of archaeological projects for Cadw and other clients, including detailed studies of the character of the registered landscapes.

9. At local level, local planning authorities in Wales have designated 514 conservation areas and a number of local authorities, e.g. Cardiff County Council, have compiled local lists of buildings considered to have value in a particular community.

10. In addition to the Historic Environment Records (HERS) held by the four non-statutory Archaeological Trusts, the Royal Commission on the Ancient and Historical Monuments of Wales maintains the National Monuments Record for Wales. Cadw has digital databases for its records of designations and Amgueddfa Cymru – National Museum Wales, has a digitised database for its collections. In recent years these three national organisations and the Welsh Archaeological Trusts have worked together to implement a Framework for Historic Environment Records in Wales. One of their intentions is to establish a common web portal to allow public access to all of these records.

The case for change

11. A consultation on heritage protection in Wales was undertaken in 2003. The consultation put forward proposals for change which were similar to those in England. However, there was a recognition that differences in policy, practice and personnel – namely the position of Cadw as an Assembly Government division and the role of Archaeological Trusts in providing support to local authorities – might require a different approach to reform.

12. Responses to the consultation generally endorsed many of the principles behind the consultation document. Respondents agreed that there was some scope for introducing greater co-ordination, clarity, openness and accountability into the current heritage protection system, and that there was some potential for confusion between current designation regimes.

13. At the same time, many of the responses stressed the specific characteristics of the Welsh heritage protection system. It was felt that, with the completion of the all-Wales listing survey; the well-advanced scheduling programme; the preparation of the Register of Historic Landscapes, Parks and Gardens; and the designation of two World Heritage Sites; most of the historic assets of Wales were protected at national level through statutory or non-statutory means, and that the quality of information available about designated assets was good.

14. With this in mind, we have developed proposals that respond to the desire for change, but which build on the strengths of the current system to develop proposals tailored to the needs of the Welsh historic environment.

The New System

Designation – what do we protect and how?

15. We will simplify the current national designation system by establishing a new unified statutory system. As in England, we will bring together the current designations of listing, scheduling and registration of historic parks and gardens into new definitions of historic buildings and sites.

16. The statutory responsibility for national designations in Wales, from May 2007, will be transferred from the National Assembly for Wales to the Welsh Assembly Government. Designation decisions will be taken in the light of the statutory criteria of 'special architectural, historic or archaeological interest', supplemented by non-statutory criteria.

17. We see no need in Wales for a major change on selection criteria. The recently completed listing survey and the well-advanced work on scheduling have been done on the basis of clear, published criteria which have evolved over time and in the light of an increased understanding of various building types. Nevertheless, we shall review the criteria to ensure that they are as transparent as possible and consult on the outcome of the review.

18. To support the existing selection criteria, we will produce non-statutory selection guides, particularly in relation to post-war structures and industrial remains, to help guide further designations and aid understanding and appreciation by setting out a context for particular building types. These guides will be made available on the internet[48].

19. We do not propose any change to the current system of grading at I, II* and II for listed buildings and registered historic parks and gardens. We shall consider further whether clarification is required to underpin these grades. We do not propose to introduce different grades for scheduled ancient monuments but see some merit in all currently scheduled monuments – and new designations – attracting a grade I classification.

[48] www.cadw.wales.gov.uk

Designation – how the system will work

20. To underpin the new statutory system of unified Welsh designation, we will introduce a new Register of Historic Sites and Buildings of Wales. This will include all currently listed buildings and scheduled ancient monuments, World Heritage Sites, registered historic parks and gardens and, if appropriate, historic battlefields. In time, this unified Register will replace the current lists, schedules and register of parks and gardens and will provide a single point of information about all nationally designated assets in Wales. This will help improve understanding of Wales' historic environment which, linked to other changes such as the developing Historic Wales web portal, will provide better ease of access to information on the historic environment of Wales for the benefit of statutory agencies, owners, amenity bodies and the general public.

21. We shall consider whether historic battlefields might form part of the new Register, in the light of the outcome of the current research, review and consultation being undertaken by the Royal Commission on the Ancient and Historical Monuments of Wales. Particular consideration will be given to whether battlefield sites in Wales are capable of being identified with sufficient precision to inform prospective planning applications.

22. Most designations in Wales are already supported by a detailed description. The majority of descriptions in Wales will therefore be transferred to the new register as they stand. However, we will update older descriptions to ensure consistency of approach and to provide local planning authorities with clear and up-to-date guidance about the significance of an item and the reason for designation. We shall also review those assets – such as bridges or major monuments – which currently have dual designations to provide a single designation only.

23. Cadw already notifies owners where it proposes to designate buildings and monuments. With appropriate safeguards to protect items from precipitate demolition, this process will be extended to a formal consultation with owners and local authorities where Cadw proposes to designate a building, monument, park or garden or archaeological site. Consultees will be given 28 days in which to provide comments.

24. To ensure openness and accountability, we shall introduce a statutory right of appeal against designation decisions in Wales. This will not be retrospective. Historic assets in Wales have been identified through survey and review and this, combined with new consultation arrangements, means that we do not envisage large numbers of statutory appeals. We do not propose therefore to establish a new independent appeals body but will consider further what arrangements might be put in place that would be quick and efficient for appellants.

Heritage protection and planning

25. Welsh unitary authorities are generally small and only three authorities and two national parks authorities currently have dedicated archaeology advisers. Applications for Scheduled Monument Consent for works to monuments are determined by the Welsh Assembly Government through Cadw. There are about 100 consent applications per year, a figure which has remained largely unchanged over recent years. Most applications are for positive works or for works with a largely neutral impact, and

many also incorporate successful applications to Cadw for grant aid or are applications from local authorities which are determined by the Welsh Assembly Government.

26. The current system has considerable strengths. Cadw has considerable and recognised expertise in relation to the archaeological resource and well-developed and efficient processes for considering and determining applications within set target times. Until local authorities develop greater skills and acquire greater capacity, we do not envisage this function being delegated. In present circumstances, a system of applications for consent to the local authorities with a call-in power for the Assembly Government offers no benefits. Statutory powers will however be framed flexibly to enable local authorities in Wales wishing to exercise responsibility over the control of works to monuments in their area to be able to do so.

27. While we do not envisage major change to the operation of the current consents system in Wales, we do feel that there is a case for some more limited changes that will enhance and clarify protection for some types of historic assets, as set out below.

Registered Historic Parks and Gardens

28. The Register of Historic Parks and Gardens in Wales was compiled on a voluntary basis and identifies parks and gardens with particular special historic interest which should be protected within the planning system. We feel that the Register would carry more weight and would be more consistent with other elements of the designation system if put on a statutory basis. We therefore intend to include registered historic parks and gardens on the new unified Register.

29. Inclusion of registered historic parks and gardens on the Register will not bring any additional statutory controls. However, separately, we will introduce the statutory consultation of Cadw, the Garden History Society and the Welsh Historic Gardens Trust, on planning applications affecting registered historic parks and gardens and their settings.

World Heritage Sites

30. The importance of protecting Wales' World Heritage Sites and their settings is set out in policy and related circular guidance.[49] We will review planning policies and guidance and set in place measures to clarify and strengthen the protection for sites and their buffer zones.

Local designations

31. Buildings of local architectural or historic interest contribute enormously to the character and appearance of our cities, towns and villages. Although they do not meet the criteria for listing, they have been a key feature in the history of local areas and are often held in great affection by the local community. In recent years growing development pressures have seen local authorities largely powerless to prevent the demolition of these distinctive buildings and there have been a number of losses.

32. We propose to bring the demolition of locally important buildings within the sphere of development control. This will do much to protect and safeguard these important and distinctive buildings which help shape our local communities. It is hoped that these changes will encourage local authorities to look again at the potential of local list designation as an important tool to its local planning policies and as a complement to national designations.

[49] Planning Policy Wales and Welsh Office Circular 61/96.

The Ecclesiastical Exemption

33. The results of the consultation exercise in Wales[50] recommended that the exempted denominations should continue to enjoy the exemption from secular controls but identified a number of areas where current arrangements could be improved. These areas will be pursued further with the denominations. We will also consider whether there is scope for the exemption to cover a wider range of assets, as is proposed for England, in consultation with the exempt denominations.

Heritage Partnership Agreements

34. Wales has a number of multi-designated sites which could benefit from the Heritage Partnership arrangements described in more detail in Part 1 of this White Paper. HPAs potentially offer considerable benefits to owners who manage properties with a number of different designated assets, potentially reducing the burdens of multiple same site applications. In Wales we will introduce HPAs on a voluntary basis along similar lines to those in England.

Characterisation

35. Historic landscape characterisation work, both in the countryside and in urban areas, has considerable potential to inform changes affecting the historic environment. This is not restricted to buildings but features such as town squares and other small open areas, town green spaces, sports facilities, allotments and planned environments all contribute to local distinctiveness. Cadw will therefore seek opportunity to broaden and develop this area of activity.

Access to information

36. We recognise the importance of clear and accessible information to support the effective management of historic assets, and most designation records in Wales are of a high quality. Under the new system, Cadw will remain responsible for maintaining definitive data for nationally designated sites.

37. Cadw's records are part of an integrated and evolving structure of records of the Welsh historic environment. The Royal Commission oversees the data standards and enhancement of those records, which are co-ordinated through the Extended National Database (END) partnership. The Commission also holds the National Monuments Records and its on-line catalogue, Coflein. This forms the primary archive for information on the Welsh historic environment. Complementary to the national records are the regional Historic Environment Records held by the four Welsh Archaeological Trusts. These records strive to provide consistent and up-to-date information on the historic environment at a more local level. The HERs are working tools which underpin the heritage management and development control advice provided to their local authorities and a wide range of other organisations and individuals.

38. As in England, we will place a statutory duty on local authorities to adopt and support HERs, either directly or through the agency of others. The existing Service Level Agreements already in place between most of the local authorities and the Welsh Archaeological Trusts provide a mechanism through which this duty could be discharged. This will ensure that local authorities can carry out their planning and other responsibilities towards the historic environment effectively.

[50] *The Howell Report.*

39. Cadw will build on the Historic Wales web portal launched in November 2006 which houses core data held by the National Monuments Record and Amgueddfa Cymru – National Museum Wales. Cadw will add its data in 2007 and other partners intend to join in future years.

3 Protecting the marine historic environment in the UK

Summary

DCMS, along with Ministers in Wales, Scotland and Northern Ireland, will develop an improved UK-wide system of marine heritage protection that can work effectively alongside national systems. To do this:

- We will broaden the range of marine historic assets that can be protected.
- Designation decisions will be made on the basis of special archaeological or historic interest.
- We will make designation decisions easier to understand by publishing new selection criteria for marine designation.
- We will introduce simpler and clearer designation records.
- We will introduce interim protection for marine historic assets.
- We will consider the scope for a new, flexible consents system, including provision for voluntary management agreements.
- We will introduce a new statutory duty on the Receiver of Wreck to inform heritage bodies about marine historic assets.

1. The marine environment includes some of our most important historic assets. Our waters contain large numbers of historic wrecks, both from the UK and abroad, reflecting our rich maritime heritage and historic patterns of international trade, exploration and conquest. Geographical changes, from the flooding of land surfaces now beneath the English Channel and the North Sea to current coastal erosion, have resulted in significant historic assets that were once on land becoming submerged.

2. Demands on our marine environment are growing. Whether for commercial exploitation, environmental protection or recreational use, there is increasing pressure on both coastal areas and territorial seas. In light of these changing demands, the Government will soon bring forward proposals for a new legislative framework for the management of activities in the marine area. The Marine White Paper will set out proposals to put in place a better system for delivering sustainable development of the marine and coastal environment, addressing both the use and protection of marine resources, while deriving sustainable economic and social benefits.

3. In order to ensure that the protection of the marine historic environment can operate more effectively in the future, we will make important changes to the current marine heritage protection system. We will review the range of marine heritage that can be protected; we will improve the designation regime and the information available about marine historic assets; we will consider the scope for a new marine consents regime; and we will increase protection for some marine historic assets. The objective will be to develop an effective marine heritage protection system, which provides appropriate protection for our historic assets, that is simple and clear, and that delivers designation decisions quickly. We will also need to ensure that the changes to the marine heritage protection system are consistent and compatible with any proposed changes to the wider marine management framework that may be brought forward through a Marine Bill, and wider changes to the heritage protection system on land.

A more comprehensive regime

4. The current marine heritage protection system enables us to designate only a narrow range of historic assets[51]. As a consequence, some important aspects of our marine heritage remain unprotected. Public consultation has shown strong support for a more flexible marine protection system that can accommodate a broader range of heritage. We will therefore bring forward legislation to enable the designation of a broader range of marine historic assets, including built structures, archaeological sites, and the sites of wrecked vehicles, vessels or aircraft.

5. Alongside a new definition of marine historic assets, we will revise the statutory criteria for designation. The new criteria will need to be sufficiently broad so that decisions can be clear, understandable and can reflect changes to our understanding of the historic environment over time. They will also need to ensure that the complex maritime and migratory history of many countries that are represented in the archaeological record in UK waters can be accounted for, as they are at present.

6. The term 'special interest' has been tested in relation to the listing of buildings and has proved to be broad and sufficiently neutral. It also avoids the problems of assigning values of national importance to a marine environment where some of the material worthy of designation is not of British origin. We will therefore introduce new statutory selection criteria of "special archaeological or historic interest" to identify marine historic assets for designation.

7. In the marine environment, the concept of assigning an age criterion for assets to qualify for designation is problematic. In particular there is the recognition that recent artefacts, especially of wrecks and aircraft, can be of great historical importance. Therefore, provided they meet the statutory criteria, there will be no age limit for marine historic assets to be considered for designation.

8. Given the complexities of use, ownership and access in the marine historic environment, discretion in designation decisions is crucial. Designation decisions will be based on the most appropriate management regime for a marine historic asset, not simply on its 'special interest' alone.

9. The difficulties of access and survey for many underwater sites mean that a grading system is likely to be impractical and over-complex. Therefore, there will be no grading regime for designated marine historic assets.

10. Marine designation will continue on a UK-wide basis. Much marine law and regulation is UK-based and public consultation has shown strong support for a continued UK-wide legislative framework for marine heritage protection. Within this UK-wide framework, DCMS and English Heritage, Scottish Ministers (through Historic Scotland), Welsh Assembly Government (through Cadw) and the Department for the Environment Northern Ireland will continue to be responsible for the protection and management of the marine historic environment in their respective administrations, with scope for using either marine or terrestrial systems in areas of overlap between land and sea[52].

[51] The 1973 Protection of Wrecks Act enables the protection of wrecked vessels of "historical, archaeological or artistic importance". In addition, a limited number of marine historic assets have been designated as Scheduled Ancient Monuments. There are currently 59 designated wrecks in UK territorial waters.

[52] Marine heritage legislation will extend from mean high water springs out to the limit of territorial waters.

11. In Northern Ireland, designation of historic wrecks will follow UK practice. In addition, some marine historic assets will be protected by scheduling under the *Historic Monuments and Archaeological Objects (NI) Order 1995.*

12. The designation system will continue to cover the territorial waters of the UK. Beyond this limit, the Government is aware of the challenges facing the protection of underwater cultural heritage and is keen to ensure that underwater archaeological projects concerning British heritage are carried out according to best practice. With this in mind, the Government has recently adopted a more co-ordinated approach to wrecks in international waters to ensure that policy is as coherent as possible and that we are able to examine cases swiftly while encouraging best archaeological practice.

A clearer system

13. We will design a more coherent and simpler system for designating marine historic assets that will improve integration between coastal and marine historic environments and will provide a more user-friendly, transparent approach for all sea-users.

Applications

14. At present, anyone can nominate a wreck for designation. This open system will continue under the new system. To make the system more efficient, applications will be made using a standard application form, which applicants will be able to submit online. All applications will be made to the relevant national heritage body (English Heritage, Historic Scotland, Welsh Assembly Government through Cadw or the Environment and Heritage Service Northern Ireland).

Consultation

15. Marine designation is arguably more complex than its land equivalents in terms of ownership, access and site stability, and the largely unexplored nature of the seabed. This complexity draws a range of parties into any designation process. It is important that the full range of sea-users and interested parties have the opportunity to comment on the suitability of a site for designation.

16. Owners and other interested parties are already consulted on designation cases under the Protection of Wrecks Act 1973. This broad consultation will continue under the new designation regime.

Interim protection

17. There is currently no protection available for marine sites that are being considered for designation. As a consequence, some sites have been damaged or salvaged once a designation application has become public but before a designation order has been put in place. Emergency designation is sometimes used to ensure swift protection of a wreck, but this usually limits opportunities for consultation. As part of our reforms, we will bring forward proposals for a system of interim protection for marine historic assets when they are being considered for designation.

Access to information

18. The marine environment has a wide diversity of users. It is important that all those with interests in designated marine historic assets, whether regulators, sea-users or commercial interests, are able to access comprehensive and understandable information on these sites.

19. In England and Wales, information on designated Marine Historic Assets will be recorded through the new Registers of Historic Sites and Buildings of England and Wales respectively, and made available on-line through the England and Wales Heritage Gateways. In Scotland, this information will be added to the database of the Royal Commission on the Ancient and Historic Monuments of Scotland and made available through the PASTMAP website (www.pastmap.org.uk). In Northern Ireland this information will be made available on the Environment and Heritage Service website. Coastal local authorities will be encouraged to incorporate information on marine historic assets into their Historic Environment Records.

The Advisory Committee on Historic Wreck Sites

20. As marine designation is arguably more complex than its land equivalents in terms of ownership, access and site stability, decisions on whether to designate marine historic assets will continue to be made by the relevant national Minister[53] based on advice from the Advisory Committee on Historic Wreck Sites (ACHWS)[54] and on archaeological investigation.

21. At the same time, the ACHWS will be tasked with a more strategic advisory role and will also be asked to provide advice, where necessary, to the UK Government on the protection and management of marine historic assets beyond territorial waters, including British wrecks in international waters.

More flexible consents

22. The marine environment is complex and changeable. The shifting nature of the seabed means that historic assets may move, may be frequently uncovered or covered, and may be extremely fragile. With this in mind, a marine protection system based on a system of consents for works is unlikely to be practical. Instead, we intend to maintain the system whereby designation outlines an area of the seabed within which activities are licensed[55].

23. Public consultation has shown that sea-users are keen for a marine heritage consent system that can deliver clearer and more consistent constraints on activities. They are also keen to see a more flexible approach that acknowledges the multiple uses of the marine environment and differences between sites in terms of vulnerability.

24. As part of a more flexible approach to the management of the marine historic environment, we will consider the scope for a system of licensing that provides a range of controls for activities in designated areas in order to reflect the management needs of a particular site. This might mean, for example, that a lithic scatter or submerged fishtrap may not always need the same level of protection as a complex wreck site and there would be scope for more activities to be allowed on less vulnerable sites.

[53] In England and Northern Ireland the Secretary of State for Culture, Media and Sport, in Scotland the Minister for Tourism, Culture and Sport, and in Wales, the Welsh Assembly Government.

[54] The name of the ACHWS will need to be revised in line with its new remit.

[55] Designation under the 1973 Act creates a restricted zone around an area of the seabed, where a wreck of historic, archaeological or artistic importance lies, and within which most access or works require a licence. Licences provide a range of conditional controls that cover visiting, survey, surface recovery and excavation and aim to ensure good diving and archaeological practice.

25. As an alternative to individual licence applications, we will also introduce provision for more flexible voluntary management agreements for sites. These will allow various stakeholders to take part in voluntary agreements which would aid better and more streamlined management of sites. As with management agreements on land, they will enable greater partnership, better planning, a reduction in individual licence applications and a more holistic approach to the needs of complex sites.

26. With a broader designation system, it is unlikely to be practical for the ACHWS to determine and monitor all licensing applications. Instead, we propose that applications for routine licences covering activities such as visiting and survey are determined by national heritage bodies, while licences that may need the most scrutiny, such as recovery and excavation licences, will continue to be scrutinised by the ACHWS. The issuing of licences will be undertaken in England by English Heritage, in Scotland by Scottish Ministers (through Historic Scotland), in Wales by Welsh Assembly Government (through Cadw) and in Northern Ireland by the Department for the Environment, Northern Ireland.

Increased protection for marine historic assets

27. Responses to public consultation suggest that many in the heritage sector think that current protections for marine historic assets are insufficient[56]. In particular, heritage organisations are critical of the way in which marine historic assets are protected under UK salvage and reporting laws.

28. UK salvage and reporting laws operate under the Merchant Shipping Act 1995. This legislation requires mandatory reporting to the Receiver of Wreck (RoW) of all wreck that is landed in the UK or recovered from UK territorial waters[57]. While it ensures the appropriate management of wreck, it has no provision for the reporting of discoveries and disturbance or the reporting of non-wreck material.

29. At the same time, the international salvage regime, which also operates under the Merchant Shipping Act 1995, provides uniform international rules, incentives and safeguards for salvage operations that ensure that the skill and efforts of salvors are financially rewarded by the owner or beneficiary of the salvaged property. A salvor is entitled to a reward for recovering wreck, or to the wreck itself in lieu of a financial reward.

30. Salvage issues are complex, but respondents to the consultation had two main criticisms of the system – first, that there is no mandatory provision for reporting of discoveries and disturbance of potential historic sites; and second, that there is no legal provision for the reporting of non-wreck material. Views on the issue were mixed, however, and there were also many who believed that the system should be retained, and that voluntary good practice could be equally as helpful in ensuring adequate levels of protection.

31. Mindful of the many complex interests and concerns of the whole range of sea-users in relation to salvage and reporting, the need for further evidence on the case for change in this area, and the forthcoming Marine White Paper, substantial change to the Merchant Shipping Act 1995 will not be pursued at this time.

[56] 45% of consultation responses, mainly from heritage organisations, believed that reform of salvage law was needed.

[57] Wreck is defined in section 255 of the Merchant Shipping Act 1995 as including "jetsam, flotsam, lagan and derelict found in or on the shores of the sea or any tidal water".

While we do not feel that the time is right for major change, however, we are proposing a change designed to improve reporting, accountability and information sharing on marine historic assets.

32. The Receiver of Wreck is currently the gateway for all reports of finds of wreck from the marine environment. She has a positive relationship with a wide range of sea-users, and is involved with education initiatives that have begun to substantially improve reporting practice. At present, her role is predominantly related to reuniting owners with their property, and she has no duty to inform heritage bodies of recoveries of wreck that she receives. In practice she often does this, but in order to ensure that reports of marine historic assets are dealt with as a priority we intend to place a new statutory duty on the RoW in relation to her duties under the Merchant Shipping Act 1995.

4 Next steps and how to respond

NEXT STEPS

1. In preparation for the implementation of the proposals set out in this White Paper we intend to seek Parliamentary time for new legislation.

2. In the meantime, we will continue to make progress on improving the heritage protection system within existing legislation and preparing for legislative change.

3. In England, we will continue to work with English Heritage to improve the listing system and develop a programme of public consultation on new designation priorities. We will also begin work to develop new selection criteria for designating historic assets under the new system. English Heritage will begin to develop new guidance on local authority historic environment services and to implement a new programme of training, support and capacity-building for local authorities and local heritage organisations.

HOW TO RESPOND

4. In addition to setting out proposals for legislative change, this White Paper also asks for views in response to three questions:

- **Question 1**
  Should Conservation Area Consent be removed as a specific consent and merged with planning permission? The merger would be combined with amendments to the Demolition Direction to ensure planning permission would be required for the demolition of an unlisted building in a Conservation Area and amendments to the General Permitted Development Order to reinstate levels of protection pre-Shimizu.
- **Question 2**
  As a means of promoting early consideration of heritage issues in large scale developments, should there be new statutory guidance promoting pre-application assessment and discussion for all major planning applications which may affect historic assets?
- **Question 3**
  As a means of providing greater certainty to developers, should the current operation of Certificates of Immunity be expanded to enable an application to be made at any time, and for a site as well as an individual building?

5. **Responses, in the form of answers to these questions, should be sent to:**

- **England**
  heritagewhitepaper@culture.gsi.gov.uk or to Leila Brosnan, Architecture and Historic Environment Division, Department for Culture, Media and Sport, 2-4 Cockspur Street, London SW1Y 5DH
- **Wales**
  matthew.coward@wales.gsi.gov.uk or to Matthew Coward, Designations Branch, Cadw, Welsh Assembly Government, Plas Carew, Units 5/7 Cefn Coed, Nantgarw Cardiff, CF15 7QQ

to arrive by 1 June 2007.

6. This document can also be accessed at the DCMS, DCLG and Cadw websites, via which responses can also be sent:
   www.culture.gov.uk
   www.communities.gov.uk
   www.cadw.wales.gov.uk

7. Unless a respondent requests otherwise, all responses will be available for public scrutiny.

8. A summary of consultation responses will be published on the DCMS, DCLG and Cadw websites.

Government Code of Practice on Consultation

9. The consultation element of this document is being carried out in accordance with the Government's Code of Practice on Consultation, available on the Cabinet Office website[58]. It meets the following six criteria:

- Consult widely throughout the process, allowing a minimum of 12 weeks for written consultation at least once during the development of the policy.
- Be clear about what your proposals are, who may be affected, what questions are being asked and the timescale for responses.
- Ensure that your consultation is clear, concise and widely accessible.
- Give feedback regarding the responses received and how the consultation process influenced the policy.
- Monitor your department's effectiveness at consultation, including through the use of a designated consultation co-ordinator.
- Ensure your consultation follows better regulation best practice, including carrying out a Regulatory Impact Assessment if appropriate.

[58] www.cabinet-office.gov.uk/regulation/consultation

Annex 1 Suggested format for new Register entry (England)

The final format for new Register entries will be agreed as part of the implementation of this White Paper, but entries are likely to follow the following format developed as part of English Heritage pilot projects.

National Grid Reference ST2288124616	**HAR numbers** TA01, TA02	**Register entry number** RE1
Title/Address Church of St Mary Magdalene		
County Somerset	**District** Taunton Deane	**Parish** Taunton

Register entry description

CONTEXT

The Church of St Mary Magdalene is Taunton's principal parish church. It stands to the east of the modern town centre, just inside the line of the early medieval town defences. It is approached via Hammet Street which was dramatically aligned on its west tower in the C18. It stands within its former burial ground, now a park-like green space with mature specimen trees and a few remaining tombs and gravestones including a late medieval chest tomb. A war memorial cross stands to the north of the church.

SUMMARY OF HISTORIC ASSETS

No	Historic Asset Record	Grade
TA01	Church of St Mary Magdalene	1
TA02	Churchyard of the church of St Mary Magdalene	2

HISTORY

Saxon

The first historical reference to Taunton is in the Anglo-Saxon Chronicle for 722, although it is by no means certain that this refers to a settlement on the site of the present town. The foundation of a minster in the mid C8 may mark the beginning of settlement at what became medieval Taunton, the origin of the present town. In the late Saxon period, the manor was developed by the kings of Wessex as an important administrative, judicial and commercial centre for the extensive Tone Vale estate which stretched from the Quantocks to the Blackdowns. By the C10 there was clear evidence that Taunton was an important town, soon with a mint.

Early Medieval
By Domesday, in 1086, there were 64 burgesses in Taunton, making it the third largest town in the county after Bath and Ilchester. Taunton was tightly, and influentially, controlled by its lords, the bishops of Winchester. It was probably in the earlier C12, under Bishops William Gyffard and then Henry of Blois, that the medieval town plan was established. Gyffard (who was also King William II's Chancellor) was responsible for the upgrading of the existing Bishops' Hall to a castle, and for the conversion of the Saxon minster into an Augustinian Priory. His successor, Henry of Blois (the king's brother, and also Abbot of Glastonbury), built the castle keep and town defences. He also moved the Priory beyond the town defences, primarily in order to relieve pressure of space on the castle, which was gradually enlarged under his successors. A borough charter was granted in 1136. It was probably at about this time that the church of St Mary Magdalene was founded. Established close to the Priory's new location but within the town defences, it presumably served as the main church for the redefined and expanding town. By the C14 Taunton was one of the largest and wealthiest towns in the county after Bath and Bristol and remained prosperous for the rest of the middle ages.

Post-medieval
The town apparently sustained much damage in the civil wars of the mid C17, and showed signs of economic decline in the C18, when the cloth industry, on which it had previously relied, waned. Its fortunes were saved by the growth of silk mills and increased communications (on the River Tone and newly constructed canals), and its wealth is demonstrated by the re-planning of parts of the town, most notably Hammet Street and The Crescent, close to the Church of St Mary Magdalene. Further industrial and commercial development was promoted by the arrival of the railway in the 1840s, which also encouraged the residential expansion of the town.

FURTHER INFORMATION

M. Aston and R. Leach, *Historic Towns in Somerset: Archaeology and Planning* (1977), 136-7

English Heritage, *Somerset: Extensive Urban Survey* (Taunton) (2002)

Other Designations
Conservation Area

Historic Asset Record Church of St Mary Magdalene			**Asset number** TA01
National Grid Reference ST2288124616	**County** Somerset	**District** Taunton Deane	**Parish** Taunton
Grade 1		**Related Records** TA02	

Summary of Historic Asset
A large medieval urban church, with fabric dating from C13 to C16 with a C19 rebuilding directed by George Gilbert Scott and a C20 extension by Martin Stancliffe.

Reason for Designation
The church of St Mary Magdalene meets the criteria for designation at grade 1 for its special architectural, historic and archaeological interest:

- it is a major late medieval town church;
- the height and architecture of the tower, accurately rebuilt in mid C19, is of particular interest as a distinctive feature of many Somerset churches. St Mary Magdalene is one of the finest in the county;
- there is evidence of a significant C13 church and high potential for below-ground archaeology relating to earlier churches on site;
- the church has an unusual plan, a nave with four aisles, creating a remarkably broad and complex interior which also contains an impressive range of C19 fittings and stained glass and monuments of note dating from the C16;
- it has had a continued presence within the townscape, from the middle ages and again after re-ordering of streets in the C18 and has significant group value with the rectory and other designated buildings in Church Square and Hammet Street.

Extent of Special Interest
The above ground structure, the interior, including fixtures and fittings, and any below-ground remains and structures are of special interest. There are two C20 extensions to the north-east of the building and these are part of the special interest of the church. The late C20 serving counter to the rear of the north aisle is not of special interest.

Historic Asset Description

HISTORY

Taunton was an important regional centre in the C12 when St Mary's is likely to have been established, initially as a dependent chapel of the newly-founded Augustinian Priory. Situated in a prominent position within the medieval walls, it later developed parochial status as the main church of a wealthy town. Evidence of an earlier church is a C13 arcade between the two north aisles, probably built as a chapel and then extended a further three bays westwards shortly after, its length probably taking into account an earlier western tower. The proportions and plan of the C12 church to which this chapel was added is still in evidence in current church, rebuilt along the same lines. The narrowness of the aisles which flank the nave, for example, is suggestive of an early rather than late medieval date.

The many piecemeal additions and rebuilding over the medieval period may have coincided with a rise in status for St Mary's: in 1308, for example, the church took on responsibility for some local chapels. The culmination of these improvements was the great rebuilding of the late C15 to early C16, an ambitious statement of civic pride and local patronage. Building was underway by 1488, funded by local merchants. The extension of the outer aisles was possibly to create chantry chapels and the remodelling of the nave and the building of the impressive tower and south porch indicate a parish of wealth and piety in equal measure. The new church, enlarged and impressive, carefully respected the scale and proportions of the earlier medieval church. The C13 north arcade was retained, possibly because an important town guild had rights over this space.

The church was refurbished in the C18, following the iconoclasm and neglect of the Reformation and Civil War periods. From this time, or perhaps earlier, the outer aisles of the nave and chancel were used as part of a large preaching area. The foundations for a new pulpit in 1707 caused a partial collapse of the nave. As well as a pulpit on the south side of the nave there were galleries and box pews, a choir screen surmounted by the royal arms, and an organ gallery at the west end. All this was swept away by a complete reordering in the 1840s carried out and funded by the High Church incumbent the Revd Dr Cottle. The entire church was fitted with pews and new liturgical furniture commissioned. Much of the work was designed to reclaim the medieval atmosphere of the interior. Concern from parishioners about this High Church direction is evidenced by the delay in completing the statues in the pulpit, designed in 1860 and not inserted until 1877. At the same time, statues, which had been destroyed in the C17, were inserted into niches in the nave, including that of the church's patron, St Mary Magdalene.

In 1858 the tower was rebuilt as an exact copy of the existing unstable medieval tower under the supervision of George Gilbert Scott and Benjamin Ferrey. The builder was Henry David of Taunton. New materials were used except for the sculptures in the west door spandrels and the fan vault, which were retained.

Further works continued in the 1860s and 1870s, including the raising of the chancel floor by two feet and the consequent raising of the piers. New glass, screens, doors and heating were installed to commemorate Queen Victoria's golden jubilee in 1887. In 1912 alterations were made to the chancel aisles – the south aisle was restored as a chapel and the north aisle provided room for an organ chamber and vestry. In the latter years of the C20 pews were removed from the west end to provide space for a shop and other visitor facilities. In the north-east corner of the church a new two storey structure by Martin Stancliffe, which incorporated earlier vestry facilities, provided space for parish facilities including lavatories.

DESCRIPTION

MATERIALS: Local sandstone with Ham Hill dressings. The 1508 extension of the outer south aisle and the new south porch are of Ham Hill ashlar and dressings.

PLAN: nave flanked by double aisles to north and south, a chancel with flanking chapels, a tall west tower, and north-east vestries.

EXTERIOR: the dominant feature is the tower, the largest and most impressive parish church tower in Somerset. On the basis of wills it is usually dated to 1488 to 1514, and was demolished and rebuilt in replica in 1858-62. It has three storeys with paired openings above the great west window, set back buttresses and decorated open tracery parapet. Striking use is made of the contrasting colours of the sandstone and the Ham Hill stone.

The window tracery is typical of late medieval Somerset perpendicular. All the elevations date from the late C14 and early C15 period, that to the north replacing a C13 wall. The two storey south porch is dated 1508. The chancel and its chapels are medieval: the former C14, the latter late C14 or early C15.

The church has three large gable ends with pitched roofs covering the nave and outer aisles. The inner aisles are covered with almost flat roofs. The chancel projects beyond its flanking aisles. The vestries to the north-east were built in 1912 and incorporated into a 2-storey structure of vestry and parish rooms in the 1990s by Martin Stancliffe Architects.

BELOW-GROUND: There is potential for below-ground archaeology relating to earlier churches on the site and for evidence of the building phases the present church has undergone. Norman or Saxon foundations were reportedly found under the chancel arch in C19. Evidence of a C12 building was also found under the current piers of the north arcade in 1952. There could also be evidence of the pre-church late Saxon and early medieval town. In addition, there will be intra-mural burials, most likely of prominent parishioners and incumbents. The area beneath the church is thus of particular sensitivity.

INTERIOR: internally the church is characterised by its unusual huge breadth – a broad nave with two narrow aisles and two outer aisles all of six bays, the latter built in stages dated to the C13, C14 and C16. The chancel, with chapels either side, has parish facilities built in the C20 attached to the north-east corner.

The nave is distinguished by its four-centred arcade arches, sculptured angel capitals to elegant perpendicular piers, a large deep clerestory and high wall niches filled with sculptures of 1877, including the large figure of St Mary Magdalene. A painted C19 inscription runs beneath the clerestory stringcourse. Other painted schemes recorded in early C19 drawings have been lost as a result of whitewashing the interior. The effect is of a lavishly funded project to totally recast an earlier out-of-date building.

The arcade to the outer north aisle is the earliest remnant of the C13 building – the piers have round cores with four attached semi-circular shafts, simply moulded capitals and round bases. The three bays to the west are slightly later in the C13 and are somewhat wider and of different stone, though the architectural details matched closely. In the late C15 the bases of the C13 arcade were remodelled on the south side so that they related aesthetically with the fashionable and lavish new nave and inner aisles. The outer south chapel was built at this time to balance the aisles visually.

Likewise, the capitals of the C14 piers of the chancel's north aisle consciously imitate those of the C13 aisle arcade. The chancel interior was stripped and whitewashed, and the floor and piers were raised by 2 feet, in 1877. A window in the west wall of the inner north aisle, later blocked up by the enlarged new west tower, was inserted sometime in the early C15.

ROOFS: The nave is surmounted by a timber king post roof decorated with angels. The aisles are covered by high quality and elaborate timber roofs c1500 – the outer aisles with coffered timber ceilings. Only the tower and the south porch have stone vaults, the former a fan vault and the latter a tierceron vault.

FIXTURES & FITTINGS: the completeness and cohesiveness of the C19 fittings is of considerable special interest. There are wooden bench pews of 1845 with square-headed Gothic ends, poppy head choir stalls, and a font and cover of 1848. The nave pews that are decorated date from the 1860s. In the aisles, the pews are labelled 'free' implying that the nave had a propriety pew system which is unusual for this date and hence of significance. The pulpit and lectern are by Benjamin Ferrey, his second pulpit for the church in limestone and marble, and are of 1868. The statues in the niches were installed in 1877.

In the chancel is an elaborate stone and marble reredos with statues, painting and gilding by G. E. Street with matching sedilia and piscine. These enhance the C19 character of the interior, and for this they are of note. The creation of St Andrew's chapel in the south chancel chapel dated from 1912. The organ vestry in the north chancel chapel dates from the same year. The royal arms of 1637, originally above the chancel step, now hangs near the parvise window.

GLASS: The east window is by Clayton and Bell and was installed in 1887 to commemorate Queen Victoria's jubilee. Although not the best work of the London firm, this window and others by them at St Mary Magdalene are nonetheless well-executed and technically of a very high quality. The west window is by Alexander Gibbs and is from 1862-4. It is of special interest in terms of quality and interest and is in excellent condition.

Fragments of medieval glass (mosaics of brightly-coloured geometric shapes), of significance for their survival, are gathered in the heads of lights in the north aisle and clerestory windows. These are not in their original location and are likely to have been reset by local glazier William Ray in c1845. Also of note is a C17 coat of arms in stained glass in the clerestory.

Also of special interest, for their historic as well as artistic importance are the Somerset Light Infantry window in the east end of the south aisle by A. L. Moore of 1912 and the First World War window in the west end of the south aisle by the school of Kempe of c1921.

The glass in the chancel clerestory is of the 1840s by William Wailes of Newcastle, one of the leading and most prolific figures of the archaeologically-motivated phase of the gothic revival. The heraldic windows in the chancel and two windows at the east end of the north aisle are also by William Wailes. The central window in the south chancel chapel is of the 1840s by William Ray and is reminiscent of the C18, the style rejected by the Ecclesiologists.

The windows in the nave aisle were designed by Wailes as the east window in the 1840s and re-sited here in the 1920s, with additional panels added below. The comparison between this and the current east window is revealing of the shifting tastes of the C19 and is of historic interest. In St Andrew's chapel, the glass is by Clayton and Bell though the heads of the lights look earlier and are stylistically similar to those of Wailes.

MEMORIALS: There are a number of significant memorials in the church dating mostly from C16 to C19. The oldest is a two-metre square freestone memorial, previously in the chancel but relocated in 1845 to the west end of the inner south aisle, with shield, helmet, crest and mantling to Thomas More (d. 1576), once owner of Taunton Priory after the Dissolution. The wall monument to Robert Gray (d. 1635) a local benefactor and founder of the East Street almshouses on the north wall of the outer north aisle is in the artisan mannerist style with a full-length representation of the man in civilian dress, one hand on breast and the other holding gloves. He looks east to the altar. Further C17 memorials are located in the south chancel chapel (Bernard Smith, mayor, and his wife, inscribed brass plaques and Joseph Allene memorial plate). There are groups of C18 monuments at the west end of the north aisle and the west end of the nave. A notable C19 monument is that in the north aisle to John Onebye Bliss, RN, lost in the sinking of the Acorn in a hurricane between Bermuda and Halifax in 1828; the segmental upper section of the tablet shows the storm and sinking. The Regimental south aisle contains a number of memorials to members of the successive light infantry regiments associated with Taunton and Somerset since the 1840s. A board listing the names of the WWI and WWII dead is on a wall at the west end of the church. This roll of honour directs readers to the memorial stone cross outside.

FURTHER INFORMATION

Somerset Record Office D/D/Cf 1858/1, faculty, specifications, plans
Society of Antiquaries of London, church plan by Wm Burgess
www.churchplansonline.org.uk for Incorporated Church Building Society
A *Pictorial Guide to St. Mary Magdalene, Taunton,* Taunton
J. Blair *The Church in Anglo-Saxon Society* (2005), 302, 365n
R. Bush *Jeboult's Taunton* (1983),
J.P. Cheshire, *The Stained Glass Windows of St Mary Magdalene's, Taunton* (leaflet, n.d., c.2000)
R. Dunning (ed) *Christianity in Somerset* (1975), 5, 32, 58
English Heritage, *Somerset: Extensive Urban Survey* (Taunton) (2002), 29, 32.
W. Leedy *Fan Vaulting: a study of form, technology and meaning* (Santa Monica) (1980)
N. Pevsner *South and West Somerset Buildings of England* (Harmondsworth) (1958, repr 1991).
The Builder, volumes 11 (1853), 310; 16 (1858), 163; 508 and 28 (1870), 216.
Church Builder, volume 2 (1863).
Somerset Record Society *Sir Stephen Gynne's Church Notes for Somerset*, volume 82 (1994)

Ownership
The incumbent of the parish of St Mary Magdalene, Taunton.

Management History
This section is intended as a place for local authorities, CCC, or English Heritage Regional teams to record applications for heritage consents or grants.

Heritage Protection History
Listing: Church of St Mary Magdalene – Ref: 269663 – grade I – 4 June 1952, amended 4 July 1975.

Scheduling: No scheduling history

Registering: No registering history

Consents and Constraints
This section will be filled out following discussion on the appropriate consent regimes for each site.

TITLE/ADDRESS Churchyard of the church of St Mary Magdalene			**Asset number** TA02
National Grid Reference ST2288124616	**County** Somerset	**District** Taunton Deane	**Parish** Taunton
Grade 2		**Related HARs** TA01	

Summary of Historic Asset
Medieval urban churchyard including its gates, gate piers, walls and railings, tombs, grave markers, a medieval chest tomb of note and a war memorial.

Reason for Designation
The churchyard meets the criteria for designation at grade 2 for its special architectural, historic and archaeological interest:

- it provides the essential setting for the church of St Mary Magdalene and the surrounding historic buildings;
- it is one of Taunton's principal historic open spaces;
- the area has archaeological potential as a burial ground since at least 1466, as part of the town defences, and for its pre C12 occupation;
- it has additional distinctive quality in the features with individual claims to special interest: boundary walls and gates to the north and west dating from the early C18 and C19 respectively, a medieval chest tomb and the war memorial.

Extent of Special Interest
All the ground defined by the churchyard walls, including above- and below-ground remains is of special interest. Late C20 path surfaces are not of special interest. The walls, gate piers and gates forming the west boundary of the churchyard, the wall forming the north boundary of the churchyard, the war memorial and the medieval chest tomb are of special interest in their own right as well as as part of the churchyard.

Historic Asset Description

HISTORY

The church stands towards the eastern end of the medieval town of Taunton, bounded to the east by the line of the medieval town defences and to the west by Church Square. The churchyard, evidenced by discovery of burials, was truncated by later urban development. Originally it stood within a larger open area of ground which was used from at least 1466, when it was granted or re-granted rights, for burials. In 1788 Hammet Street was carved out of the western half of the burial ground, and aligned axially with the west tower of the church.

In the 1840s, as part of the church's restoration, the churchyard ground level was lowered by three feet to reduce dampness. Between 1842 and 1847 specimen trees were planted and paths laid out. The churchyard was closed for burials in 1854. About 1863 railings were installed around the west and south sides of the churchyard. Responsibility for the churchyard's upkeep passed to the District Council in 1947. Most of the old headstones have been removed or re-sited since then.

DESCRIPTION

BOUNDARIES: The churchyard is roughly square; its boundaries have been unchanged since at least 1890. To the west the churchyard is bounded by a low stone wall which stands close to the church and angles around it. Rising from this are piers between which run elaborate iron railings, of particular special interest (see below). Originally the wall and railings also formed the south churchyard boundary; piers and railings have been removed leaving only the low stone wall.

The north boundary is a brick wall, about 2m high, a feature of particular note (see below). The north half of the east churchyard boundary is a 2.5m high brick wall of similar character to that bounding it to the north. At its north end tall C18 brick piers with stone ball-caps and iron gates with overthrow. The right-hand pier was rebuilt in late C20 and the gates are of similar date and not of historic interest although they provide an attractive, formal entrance to the churchyard. At the south end of this section of wall is a doorway with arched head. The remainder of the boundary is formed by the end wall of a building extending to the north.

BELOW-GROUND: The east boundary of the churchyard abuts the line of the bank-and-ditch town defences which remain upstanding in the vicarage grounds to the north and are of special archaeological interest. The town defences are first documented 1158, although it is not impossible that the line was established in the late Saxon period. There may have been modification of the defences during the Civil

Wars of the mid C17 when Taunton was besieged. The area of the churchyard boundary may overlie the tail of the defensive bank, which itself may overlie occupation or other evidence sealed when the defences were constructed.

The churchyard will also contain the buried remains, generally east-west inhumations, of parishioners dating from at least the middle ages. Exceptionally, they will be accompanied by grave markers, coffins or other material remains relating to burial customs. If excavation were unavoidable, large recovered samples of these would have the potential to reveal information about the health, diet, lifestyles and customs of past populations, of considerable archaeological significance. Moreover, the ground beneath the churchyard has special historic interest as a place which has been in continuous use, and considered sacred, for many centuries. As God's Acre, it is the final resting place of those people whose remains lie below, with some of the later individuals identified on their tombstones.

FEATURES: Photographs show the churchyard before its partial clearance after 1947. The few remaining headstones and tombs are important reminders of the area's history and contribute significantly to the setting. The earliest surviving monument, of the early C16, stands south-east of the church. There are a few monuments of about 1790 to 1830 with good lettering, and a large one of about 1850 to the north and east of the church.

There are 4 features of particular note:

- **War memorial cross on a plinth and three-stepped base**

In the style of a churchyard cross of the late Middle Ages, the war memorial is of ashlar and comprises an elaborate foliate cross head set on a tapering, angular, shaft. This rises from a square plinth, each face of which carries a well executed carving in relief showing symbols associated with the Passion. The plinth stands at the top of an octagonal base, rising in three steps. The memorial carries an inscription on a step which reads:

To the glory of Christ crucified / To the memory of the men who made the great sacrifice / in the World War 1914-1918 / Their name / liveth / for evermore

The second step has an inscription which reads:
They nobly played their part / They heard the call / for God for King for Country / they gave their all.

The memorial was erected soon after the end of the First World War to commemorate the sacrifice of the parishioners of St Mary Magdalene during the conflict. A memorial listing the names of the dead was erected inside the church at the same time. This roll of honour directs readers to the stone cross outside.

- **Walls, gate piers and gates forming west boundary of churchyard**

All in a loosely late gothic style, dating from 1863. The double wrought-iron gates have scrollwork above and multi-foiled motifs below the crossbar. The gate-piers with gates come forward in centre. Running back to the left and right are low stone walls surmounted by wrought-iron scrolled railings divided at regular intervals by square ashlar piers with crenellated tops and pinnacles. A second set of wrought-iron gates with similar detail stands to the north. A further gateway without gates is opposite the south porch.

- **Wall forming north boundary of churchyard**

The wall is of C17 or early C18 date. Largely of brick, it becomes of rubble stone midway along the north side of the churchyard where it doglegs. Towards the north-east corner of the churchyard it doglegs again and has been rebuilt in brick (incorporating a garage façade set in an earlier building) in the late C20. The modern brick wall and garage façade are not of special interest. At the west end of the north wall is an elaborate brick-and-stone gateway giving access to the Vicarage grounds. Probably of C16 date, it has a carved coat of arms set in its pediment, but has been heavily restored in C19 and C20.

- **Chest tomb to the south east of the church**

Made of white limestone, this is a large free-standing tomb chest with overhanging slab. The sides of the chest are divided into three decorated panels by (partially damaged and eroded) buttresses, standing on a moulded plinth. Each panel comprises two quatrefoils enclosing sculptured features, set beneath a large cinquefoil panel. The mouldings of the chest are integral with the existing slab, the underside of which itself is decorated with tablet flowers or fleurons. No inscriptions are legible. The style of the tomb indicates a late medieval date. It is likely this was the grave of a wealthy townsman.

PLANTING: Standing in the east half of the churchyard is a number of coniferous and deciduous trees including a Wellingtonia, pines and yews, mostly dating from the 1840s landscaping. These contribute to the setting of the church and the special interest of the churchyard as a historic open space in the centre of the town.

FURTHER INFORMATION

R. Bush, 1983 *Jeboult's Taunton* (Buckingham 1983), frontispiece, 50, 55

English Heritage, *Somerset: Extensive Urban Survey* (Taunton) (2002), 26-7

Ownership

The incumbent of the parish of St Mary Magdalene, Taunton

Management History

This section is intended as a place for local authorities, CCC, or English Heritage Regional teams to record applications for heritage consents or grants.

Heritage Protection History

Listing: Gates and piers with railings at west end of Church of St Mary Magdalene – Ref: 269664 – grade II – 4 July 1975

Scheduling:No scheduling history

Consents and Constraints

This section will be filled out following discussion on the appropriate consent regimes for each site

Annex 2 Proposed operation of Historic Asset Consent (HAC)

Control of works	• It will be an offence for any person to execute or cause to be executed any works for the demolition or destruction of a Registered Building and Archaeological Site or for its alteration of extension in any manner which would affect its special architectural, archaeological or historic interest unless the works are authorised.
Authorisation of works	• Local planning authorities, the Secretary of State for Communities and Local Government and the Welsh Assembly Government will be empowered to grant written consent for the execution of works to or the demolition of Registered Buildings and Archaeological Sites.
Unauthorised works	• It will be an offence to carry out any unauthorised work to a Registered Building or Archaeological Site. • There will be a defence that works to the Registered Building or Archaeological Site were urgently necessary in the interests of safety or health or for the preservation of the registered asset, that works were limited to the minimum measures immediately necessary, and that notice in writing is given to the local planning authority as soon as reasonably practical. • The defence of ignorance that the area was scheduled in relation to unauthorised works to a Scheduled Ancient Monument will be removed for works to Registered Buildings and Archaeological Sites.
Penalties for offence	• A sentence of imprisonment will be available as a penalty for this offence, both on summary conviction and conviction on indictment. • The fine for a summary conviction of a person found guilty of an offence will be harmonised at £20,000, with an unlimited fine for conviction on indictment. • In determining the amount of any fine, the court may take into consideration any financial benefit which accrues or is likely to accrue in consequence of the offence.
Class consents	• The Secretary of State for Communities and Local Government and the Welsh Assembly Government may grant class consents for particular types of work to Registered Buildings and Archaeological Sites.
Applications	• Applications for works to Registered Buildings and Archaeological Sites in England will be made to and dealt with by the local planning authority. • Plans and drawings will be required for all HAC applications.

Duty to refer application to SofS / Welsh Assembly Government	• The SofS for Communities and Local Government and the Welsh Assembly Government will be empowered to give directions requiring applications for Historic Asset Consent to be referred to him/it instead of being dealt with by the local planning authority
Duty to notify SofS / Welsh Assembly Government / the Commission of applications	• The specific cases in which local planning authorities will be required to notify will be set out in detail in secondary legislation
Considering applications	• Applicants and owners will be given the opportunity to make representations to the local planning authority in relation to a consent application. • Consultation arrangements for consent will be set out in secondary legislation. LPAs will be required to consult with national amenity societies. • There will be no power to hold a public local enquiry or hearing in relation to consent applications
Conditions	• Local planning authorities, the Secretary of State and Welsh Assembly Government may grant consent applications subject to conditions.
Duration of consent	• The duration of any consent will be three years.
Enforcement	• Enforcement measures will be harmonised.
Appeals	• Applicants for Historic Asset Consent will be able to appeal to the Secretary of State for Communities and Local Government and the Welsh Assembly Government if they are aggrieved by the decision of the local planning authority, if the local planning authority has failed to determine the application. • Appeals relating to Historic Asset Consent will be heard by the Planning Inspectorate.
Urgent works	• LPAs, the Secretary of State and the Welsh Assembly Government will have powers to execute urgent works to Registered Buildings and Archaeological Sites.
Compulsory purchase	• The Secretary of State for Communities and Local Government, Welsh Assembly Government and local planning authorities will have powers of compulsory acquisition.
Compensation	• There will be no compensation for refusal of consent. There will be provision for compensation for revocation of consent.

Annex 3 HPR steering, stakeholder and working groups

HERITAGE PROTECTION REVIEW STEERING COMMITTEE

Geoffrey Wilson (Chair)	Equity Land Ltd
Emma Brown (Secretary)	Department for Culture, Media and Sport
Peter Beacham	English Heritage
Steve Bee	English Heritage
Robin Broadhurst	Sir Robert McAlpine Ltd
Graham Davis	Department for Communities & Local Government
David Fursdon	Country Land and Business Association
Tom Hassall	Advisory Committee on Historic Wreck Sites
Nick Johnson	Cornwall County Council
The Very Rev Keith Jones	Dean of York
Harry Reeves	Department for Culture, Media and Sport
John Sell	Joint Committee of National Amenity Societies
Yasmin Shariff	Dennis Sharp Architects
Les Sparks	Commissioner of English Heritage & CABE
Ron Spinney	Rockspring Property Investment Managers Ltd
Peter Studdert	Cambridgeshire Horizons Ltd

HERITAGE PROTECTION REVIEW STAKEHOLDER GROUP

Frances MacLeod (Chair)	Department for Culture, Media and Sport
John Tallantyre (Secretary)	Department for Culture, Media and Sport
Malcolm Airs	Institute of Historic Building Conservation
Dave Barrett	Assoc. of Local Government Archaeological Officers
Dave Batchelor	English Heritage
Peter Beacham	English Heritage
Tim Boulding	Department for Environment, Food & Rural Affairs
Emma Brown	Department for Culture, Media and Sport
Stewart Bryant	Assoc. of Local Government Archaeological Officers
Dave Chetwyn	Royal Town Planning Institute
Kate Clark	Heritage Lottery Fund
Nigel Clubb	English Heritage

Simon Edwards	Department for Communities and Local Government
Peter Hinton	Institute of Field Archaeologists
Bob Hook	English Heritage
Vicky Hunns	Rural Development Service
Claudia Kenyatta	Department for Culture, Media and Sport
Ged Lawrenson	Planning Officers Society
Duncan McCallum	English Heritage
Sean O'Reilly	Institute of Historic Building Conservation
Kate Pugh	Heritage Link
Lee Searles	Local Government Association
Matthew Slocombe	Joint Committee of National Amenity Societies
Roger Stratton-Smith	Department for Culture, Media and Sport

MARINE REVIEW WORKING GROUP – DEFINITIONS AND DESIGNATIONS

Gordon Barclay (Chair)	Historic Scotland
Lizzie West (Secretary)	Department for Culture, Media and Sport
Dr Colin Breen	University of Ulster
Laura Forster	Department for Culture, Media and Sport
Robin Daniels	ALGAO
Sophia Exelby	Receiver of Wreck
Antony Firth	Wessex Archaeology
Dr Carolyn Heeps	The Crown Estate
Paul Jeffrey	English Heritage
Claudia Kenyatta	Department for Culture, Media and Sport
Peter McDonald	Ministry of Defence
Emily Musson	Department for Environment, Food & Rural Affairs
Dr Chris Pater	English Heritage
Dr Sian Rees	Cadw

MARINE REVIEW WORKING GROUP – SALVAGE AND REWARD

Tom Hassall (Chair)	Advisory Committee on Historic Wreck Sites
Lizzie West (Secretary)	Department for Culture, Media and Sport
Sophia Exelby	Receiver of Wreck
Patrick Griggs	Retired Secretary, British Maritime Law Association
Michael Laurie	BMT Salvage
Alan Saville	National Museums of Scotland
Dr Carolyn Heeps	The Crown Estate
Jan Gladysz	Department for Transport
Robert Yorke	Joint Nautical Archaeology Policy Committee
David Gaimster	Society of Antiquaries of London
Mike Palmer	Site Licensee
Ian Oxley	English Heritage
Dr Roger Bland	Portable Antiquities Scheme
Jim Spooner	Department for Transport
Michael Williams	University of Wolverhampton
Laura Warren	Department for Culture, Media and Sport

Annex 4 List of abbreviations and acronyms

AAI	Area of Archaeological Interest
ACHWS	Advisory Committee on Historic Wreck Sites
ALGAO	Association of Local Government Archaeological Officers
BPN	Building Preservation Notice
BVPI	Best Value Performance Indicator
CABE	Commission for Architecture and the Built Environment
CAC	Conservation Area Consent
CPA	Comprehensive Performance Assessment
DCLG	Department for Communities and Local Government
DCMS	Department for Culture, Media and Sport
DEFRA	Department for Environment, Food and Rural Affairs
DfT	Department for Transport
DoENI	Department of the Environment Northern Ireland
EH	English Heritage
GPDO	General Permitted Development Order
HAC	Historic Asset Consent
HAR	Historic Asset Record
HELM	Historic Environment Local Management
HER	Historic Environment Record
HPA	Heritage Partnership Agreement
HPR	Heritage Protection Review
IFA	Institute of Field Archaeologists
IHBC	Institute of Historic Building Conservation
LA	Local Authority
LBC	Listed Building Consent
LDF	Local Development Framework
LPA	Local Planning Authority
MHA	Marine Historic Asset
NMR	National Monuments Record
ODPM	Office of the Deputy Prime Minister
PAS	Portable Antiquities Scheme
PPG	Planning Policy Guidance
PPS	Planning Policy Statement
REIA	Race Equality Impact Assessment
RHBSE	Register of Historic Buildings and Sites of England
RIA	Regulatory Impact Assessment
RoW	Receiver of Wreck
SMC	Scheduled Monument Consent
SofS	Secretary of State
SofSCLG	Secretary of State for Communities and Local Government
SofSCMS	Secretary of State for Culture, Media and Sport
UNESCO	United Nations Educational, Scientific and Cultural Organisation
WHS	World Heritage Site

Printed in the UK for The Stationery Office Limited
on behalf of the Controller of Her Majesty's Stationery Office
ID5527993 03/07

Printed on Paper containing 75% fibre content minimum.